The Complete Kitchen Garden

The Complete Kitchen Garden

AN INSPIRED COLLECTION OF GARDEN DESIGNS AND 100 SEASONAL RECIPES

Ellen Ecker Ogden
co-founder of The Cook's Garden

Illustrations by Ramsay Gourd
Photographs by Ali Kaukas

Stewart, Tabori & Chang
New York

Published in 2011 by Stewart, Tabori & Chang
An imprint of ABRAMS

Library of Congress Cataloging-in-Publication Data

Ogden, Ellen.
The complete kitchen garden / Ellen Ecker Ogden.
    p. cm.
ISBN 978-1-58479-856-9 (alk. paper)
1. Kitchen gardens. 2. Vegetable gardening. I. Title.
SB321.O335 2010
635—dc22
                              2010032448

Editor: **Dervla Kelly**
Designer: **Pamela Geismar**
Production Manager: **Ankur Ghosh**

The text of this book was composed in Scala, Archer,
and Sketch Block

Printed and bound in U.S.A.
10 9 8 7 6 5 4 3 2 1

Stewart, Tabori & Chang books are available at special
discounts when purchased in quantity for premiums
and promotions as well as fundraising or educational
use. Special editions can also be created to specification.
For details, contact specialsales@abramsbooks.com or
the address below.

ABRAMS
THE ART OF BOOKS SINCE 1949

115 West 18th Street
New York, NY 10011
www.abramsbooks.com

Dedicated to my children Molly and Sam,
the next generation of gardeners.

Contents

9   From Art to the Kitchen Garden

13   Getting Started

14   Why a Kitchen Garden?

16   How to Get Started

35   Kitchen Gardens

37   The Salad Lover's Garden

53   The Organic Rotation Garden

67   The Cook's Garden

81   The Children's Garden

95   The Culinary Herb Garden

109   The Paint Box Garden

123   The Patio Garden

137   The Heirloom Maze Garden

151   The Garnish Garden

165   The Chef's Garden

179   The Family Garden

195   The Artist's Garden

209   The Country Garden

221   The Four Friends Garden

237   Resources

238   Designing a Kitchen Garden

240   Preserving the Bounty

243   A Well-stocked Pantry

245   Recipe Index

250   Plant Index

252   Index

255   Acknowledgments

From Art to the Kitchen Garden

I planted my first garden in 1980, marking the perimeters with four sticks and a ball of twine. With a sharp-edged spade, I removed a thick layer of rugged turf, dug up the stony soil to create a reasonably loose pile, then shoveled on some compost. Using the same four sticks and twine, I measured out long, straight rows before planting seeds for basil, lettuce, and arugula. I sprinkled them with water and walked away. I was fresh out of art school and just starting a small design business. I thought this might be a good way to feed myself.

I would be stretching the truth if I said the garden thrived. There was a constant battle with the weeds, and the garden hose didn't quite reach, so the plants were frequently thirsty. Yet the thrill of dashing to the garden just before dinner to clip a few leaves of frilly Lolla Rossa and crimson Bull's Blood beet greens for my salad kept me at it. And that thrill gave way to a feeling of pride in growing my own food. I reveled in fewer trips to the grocery store in favor of wandering into the garden with bare feet and a harvest basket. This set in motion the creation of a larger patch the following year, with my husband, and soon our garden covered almost an acre. Since we could buy tomatoes, corn, and cucumbers at the market, but couldn't always find tender loose-leaf lettuce, baby spinach, piquant sweet basil, or savory fennel leaves for spicing up our salad bowl, we focused on growing crops that were hard to find, with a fragile shelf life, so the time between the garden and the table was always kept to just a few minutes before dinner.

The garden took up more and more of my time; eventually, instead of making art on a canvas, I began to think of myself as a food artist. I built a collage of lettuces splashed with dabs of red orache, fronds of chervil, and rosettes of claytonia. Seeds and plants were my paintbrush, as I combined waves of bronze-tipped lettuce with swirls of magenta radicchio and spikes of blue-green kale, highlighted with accents of brilliant orange nasturtiums. The long, straight rows gave way to fancy arcs and geometric triangles, and I began to look for inspiration from classic European-style kitchen gardeners, with recipes to match.

It wasn't long before my husband and I were in search of a wider variety of ornamental edibles and began to import seeds for chicories and onions from Italy, mache from Switzerland, along with heirloom lettuce and mesclun from France. Along the way, we discovered seventeenth-century seed recipes for mesclun mixes originally created by French and Italian gardeners for their own kitchen gardens, with fitting names that reflected their origins: Provencal, Misticanza, and Nicoise. We couldn't get enough of them, and began to order seeds in five-kilo bags. Clearly, our garden project had progressed well beyond growing a few things to eat. So in 1984, we cofounded a seed catalog called The Cook's Garden, to share our love of European and American heirloom lettuce and salad greens with other gardeners (as well as to justify our buying habits). At first it was just a seasonal business—during the winter, seed envelopes were packed at the kitchen counter, and during the summer, our weekend farm stand overflowed with produce from our gardens.

The seed catalog started as a two-page listing featuring close to 150 different types of exotic lettuce and fancy salad greens with wonderful foreign names—such as Reine des Glaces, Merveille de Quatre Saisons, Brussels Winter Chervil, and Osaka Purple Mustard—that were relatively unknown to American gardeners at the time. Yet we quickly discovered that there were other gardeners who, just like us, were hungry for something out of the ordinary and who shared the desire to plant a vegetable garden with a style that reflected a conscious, connected lifestyle, rather than simply a source of food.

A kitchen garden may be just a fancy name for a vegetable garden located near a kitchen door, filled with tender greens, aromatic herbs, and select fruits that are harvested on a daily basis. Yet it can also be a way of life. A successful kitchen garden engages all of the senses through a rich tapestry of colors, fragrance, and ultimately, flavors. When you cultivate a kitchen garden, you actively engage with your source of food and integrate with your natural surroundings in a way that far surpasses the experience of purchasing food at the market. Growing your own food is truly the next logical step beyond "local."

In 2009, when the Obama family planted a kitchen garden at the White House, it reignited a trend that had been largely dormant for the past century. The simple act of tilling up the lawn and sowing seeds inspired thousands of families to dig up their own backyards and plant vegetable gardens. This return to our agricultural roots resonated with what Thomas Jefferson once declared the noblest pursuit: farming. The Obamas set the stage for Americans to rediscover the simple pleasures of growing their own food as a welcome alternative to the high cost of packaged foods purchased in supermarkets.

Setting an example is one of the best ways we can effect positive change. When we bring our families together around the table to share our love for good homegrown food, we are cultivating a healthy choice that spreads beyond our own backyard. Teaching basic skills such as how to build a compost pile to keep waste out of landfills, how to encourage natural pollinators like honeybees, and how to cook with simple, whole foods harvested seasonally may seem like small steps, but when we learn to become responsible consumers, we also reclaim our health as a nation.

It's been thirty years since I planted my first kitchen garden. Now I find it easier to start the plan on a large piece of graph paper, and then map out the space with a stick and a ball of twine. I limit my wish list of seeds and plants to only the foods I can't buy at the local farmers' markets, and while I have my favorites, I try planting something new each year that will surprise me and challenge the way I cook.

My kitchen garden has evolved into more than a place to grow beautiful food, and it gives me immense satisfaction to know that I am part of the natural cycle of seasons that make up a year in the garden. From the first early spears of asparagus that shoot up through the soil to the final spreading of compost on the garden beds in the fall, I revel in the privilege of growing my own food and in the connection I have to my land and the wonders of its soil.

Ellen Ecker Ogden

Getting Started

Why a Kitchen Garden?

Sowing seeds and watching food grow goes
back to the first hunter-gatherers, yet the earliest documented form of
orderly kitchen gardens were the ancient Persian gardens from around
1500 BCE. This type of garden, called a Paradise garden, was located
within a walled enclosure at the center of a home, and formed an
outdoor room for entertaining, contemplation, and listening to poetry
or music. The Paradise garden sheltered a vibrant collection of fruits
and flowering plants, and always included a water feature in the form
of a central fountain that split the garden into four squares symbolizing
the four nourishing liquids found in Paradise: milk, honey, wine, and
water. Each garden plot represented the four cardinal directions: North,
South, East, and West. The Paradise garden style was adopted by the
Greeks and Romans, and continued to be a source of culinary as well as
aesthetic enjoyment.

During the Medieval era and the fall of the Roman Empire, anything that was considered sensual and pleasurable, which included
beautiful gardens, was banned. Monasteries became the disseminators
of the church doctrine; kitchen gardens were grown behind high walls
and colonnades of tall trees, and were largely the domain of the monks
and nuns. They cultivated a much simpler style of garden than was
previously enjoyed, focusing on useful medicinal or culinary plants for
the benefit of the community. Yet like their Persian precursors, these
gardens were laid out in intricately patterned beds with espaliered pear
trees, climbing vines, and vegetables planted in geometric grids. These
monastery gardens served as a retreat for meditation and prayer, as
well as a primary source of nourishment.

In turn, many of the features of these early medieval gardens
inspired the gardeners of the Renaissance era. The fanciful parterre
garden—featuring clipped yew, boxwood, and herbs planted in ornate
patterns—was developed, and the Baroque period took this idea even

further, giving birth to the kitchen gardens at Château de Villandry, best known as France's archetypal *potager*. Villandry featured seemingly endless geometric parterres edged in immaculately clipped boxwood to create subdivisions for ornamental vegetables and flowers. French and Italian gardeners continued to plant kitchen gardens, and their passion for fresh cuisine has inspired Americans to savor the glorious connection between the garden and the dining table.

In this book you will find a range of kitchen garden designs that bridge the old with the new, building on the classic four-square concept, along with gardens that have contemporary appeal. A kitchen garden goes beyond the simple, straight rows of a vegetable garden to combine art and cuisine in ways that enhance the experience of growing food.

How to Get Started

Gardeners can always learn from other gardeners, and I'll admit that some of my best ideas have come from visiting other gardens. All gardeners are artists, and it's a bit of a mystery the way we can start with the same materials—seeds, plants, and soil—yet the results are always different. When I plant my lettuce in waves, I think back to a neighbor who painted the landscape from her upstairs window, blending all the patterns together into a patchwork of colors. The tall bamboo teepees at the entrance to my garden for my favorite purple pole beans, Trionfo Violetto, were inspired by a trip to Italy. Edible nasturtiums ramble through my garden, reminiscent of the garden at Giverny, where Monet filled the paths with these brilliant orange, yellow, and mahogany flowers. But when it comes to learning technique, only personal experience will suffice. Like cooking or any of the arts, once a basic foundation of garden skills is established, confidence will follow.

If this is your first garden, take time to study your backyard; follow the direction of the sun and how it moves across the sky in summer and the winter. Watch when a heavy wind blows to establish if you need wind blocks, and notice where the rain collects after a storm to see if you need to create better drainage. While you build your garden, find time to step back and allow your muse to guide you in creating a garden that is as beautiful as a painting and brings in elements that establish your own personal style. This might include ornamental sculpture, espaliered fruit trees, or a simple stone bench. Before sowing seeds, take a pointed stick to draw in the soil and visualize how the plants will fill in together as they grow. This will help you figure out how much room to allow between plants, and where to plant based on their heights. Think of your garden as a blank canvas for ideas.

A kitchen garden goes beyond the simple straight rows of an ordinary garden, to encompass a balance of color, texture, and form that

is extraordinary. A true kitchen garden opens your senses in new and inspiring ways, both in the garden and in the kitchen. Plan to keep a sketchbook of ideas and to take notes and photographs to guide you from year to year, learning as you go. You'll be amazed how much information you can gather from simply observing and exploring the connections that allow all the elements in a garden to work together as a whole.

In this book you will find my own designs along with techniques and organic gardening methods to get you started. I expect you to adapt to fit your own style, your individual landscape, and your personal appetite, because there is always so much more to learn on your own. Plan to visit other gardens, but keep exploring ways to create a kitchen garden that expresses your own personality. Enjoy the process as much as the harvest, because both are equally important.

Step One: Soil

Soil is the most important component to a successful garden. Before you sow seeds or transplant seedlings, be sure your soil is rich in nutrients, weed free, and will allow roots to expand. Soil is a living, breathing organism and provides the nourishment that allows roots, shoots, and fruits to mature. While most soil contains the basic elements that plants need to grow, these elements are not always in the right proportions. Understanding how all the elements work together to produce the right balance will help you to build a natural blend of nutrient-rich soil that will keep your plants in good health.

Every region of the country has a different soil type, and learning about the soil in your region may help you understand what approach to take in your garden. Start by taking a close look at the texture and composition of your garden soil. Soil is classified according to the size of its mineral particles, and can range from coarse gravel to fine gravel, coarse sand to fine sand, and silt. Each has its own attributes that will affect the growth of your plants. To get a sense of what kind of soil you have in your garden, squeeze a clump in your hand. If it crumbles or runs through your fingers easily, your soil may be sandy. Sandy soil warms up early in the spring, drains easily, and is aerated, so roots expand easily, yet it has no capacity to hold moisture, which means that nutrients will leach out. If your soil clump holds together firmly, it may be clay, which is dense and will hold water and nutrients, but can easily become waterlogged. The ideal blend is sandy loam, which combines the lightness of sand with the nutrients of fertile soil. Sandy loam soil will resemble a piece of dense chocolate cake when gently pressed into a ball.

Maintaining healthy soil is an ongoing process, which involves spreading compost and adding organic fertilizer in the spring and the fall, as well as planting cover crops that will naturally build up nutrients in your soil when edible crops are not growing. Adding aged compost to your kitchen garden will give your soil extra vigor and vitality, as well as encourage beneficial worms and microorganisms to flourish.

Be sure to keep the soil weed free for optimum fertility, and regularly cultivate in-between rows to aerate the roots of the plants.

Garden Tip: Soil Test Kits

Soil tests are optional for the home gardener, but they are a good idea, for several reasons. A soil test is easy to do and will help you figure out what quantities of fertilizer and other soil amendments to add to fortify your plants for the growing season. New gardens will especially benefit from testing topsoil for any heavy metal residuals and to make sure that the proportions of soil amendments are adequate for your crops. You can buy soil test kits, though they are not as reliable as tests that are offered through your state's USDA extension service.

Step Two: Compost

Compost is the recycling of naturally decomposing materials to provide nutrients to your garden soil. Added to your garden at the start of the growing season and again in the fall, compost feeds your plants a blend of organic fertilizer—for free!

What can I turn into compost? It is easy to keep a bucket next to your kitchen sink to collect eggshells, coffee grounds, banana peels, old bread, and other kitchen scraps for a compost pile. Add to this spent garden plants, raked leaves, and grass clippings. Avoid meat, dairy, and other animal-based products.

How do I make a compost pile? If you can make lasagna, you will be able to follow a recipe for compost. The most important thing to remember is to create both wet and dry layers, as well as green and brown ingredients. Start with a bottom layer of twigs or old sunflower stems to allow air to flow up from beneath. Keep the compost covered, to prevent the neighborhood dogs from visiting and moisture from building up. Gardening and basic yard maintenance generate plenty of material, so find a place for both a hot and a cold compost pile.

When is compost ready? When the compost is ready, it should look like soil and smell sweet. When you squeeze a sample in your hand, it should form a loose clump. There should be no large clumps, but plenty of worms.

The Hot Fast Method: This method is contained in a bin and layered with equal portions of high-nitrogen greens (grass clippings, plant cuttings, fruit and vegetable scraps) and browns (fallen leaves, twigs, wood chips, and shredded paper) in order for the materials to properly cook. Bacteria are responsible for breaking down food scraps, and are especially active when combined with fresh air. Ideally, the compost will heat to 120°–160°F to create a natural composting action. Maintaining a high temperature is a critical element for rapid composting, and can be checked by using a compost thermometer or feeling the warmth with your hand when you turn the pile. Proper layering techniques and turning the pile every other week to keep the oxygen flowing will result in compost within three to six months.

The Cold Slow Method: This method requires less science, but it can take up to one or two years for everything to fully decompose. Spent garden plants, weeds, old potted plants, and small twigs are layered with leaves, grass clippings, and wood ash in a loose, open pile. Instead of actively turning this pile, as with the hot method, allow the plants to decompose slowly. In fact, it's best not to turn this pile more than several times a year. The advantage of this method is that you can incorporate all of your yard waste, resulting in a larger quantity of finished compost for your garden. This method may require sifting the compost through a large mesh screen in order to remove stones and other debris that may not fully break down.

Step Three: Seeds

A true kitchen garden is built on a wide range of vegetables, fruits, flowers, and herbs. Knowing what to grow and when to start seeds indoors versus sowing them directly in the garden takes a bit of experience. My own kitchen gardens contain varieties that are not commonly available in garden centers, and each spring, I order fresh seeds from seed catalogs. I have my favorite varieties, but I make a wish list that combines a balance of both "tried and true" and "new and different" varieties to keep the garden fresh.

Seed catalogs are designed to charm the gardener with color photographs. Instead of being seduced by the pictures, learn to read the copy when you are deciding what to order. Look for helpful information such as tips for sowing seeds indoors, the number of days to maturity, descriptions of height, sun or partial-shade requirements, and ideal soil conditions for that plant. Most important (if you're choosing seeds that will grow into something edible), what does it taste like? After all, you are growing a culinary garden and knowing that the variety you are planting will be the best tasting should be the ultimate goal. Don't simply settle for the ordinary—go for the flavor.

When your seeds arrive, set up a planting chart based on how long each plant will take to reach maturity and whether the seeds can be planted directly in the garden or should be started early indoors. Planting dates will vary widely across the country; when you start your seeds, be sure you know your region's frost-free date. Many long-season crops,

such as onions, and peppers, can be planted six to eight weeks before the frost-free date, while tomatoes, squash, and fruiting crops should be planted four weeks before this date. Lettuce, peas, and other cool-weather-loving crops can be sown directly in the garden as soon as the soil is prepared.

Each seed variety will germinate at a different range of requirements, but most vegetables require a simple process: Fill plug trays or small pots with fine potting soil, moisten the soil, and press the seeds in to a depth of one and one-half times the size of the seed. Cover with loose potting soil, and gently press so the seeds make contact with the soil. Keep the soil moist and warm until the seeds germinate, then move into a location with full sun or place under grow lights, until the plants are ready to transplant into the garden.

Seeds can also be sown directly in the garden; the process is the same. Mark your rows with a stick and make a straight line with twine. Sprinkle the seeds into the soil, allowing several inches in between. Cover the seed with fine soil, press gently, and water. Germination will vary depending on the season and the variety, but most seeds will germinate within three to ten days. If necessary, thin the rows to allow each plant enough room to grow to full size.

You can collect your own seeds by selecting heirloom varieties and allowing the plants to produce seedpods. Harvest in the fall and keep seeds in a cool, dry location. Plant them again for next year's garden or pass them along to friends.

Step Four: N-P-K

As compost breaks down, it will release micronutrients in proper quantities to create nutritionally rich humus, making a lasting contribution to soil nutrition and overall structure. Yet sometimes plants need more of a boost. In fact, plants require sixteen different elements in order to grow, and bagged fertilizer provides three basic building blocks. These work quickly and will give your plants a powerful boost in the short term. Since you are growing food, be sure to select an organic fertilizer rather than a chemical mix.

Each bag will be marked with three numbers separated by hyphens, which are always in the same order and represent the percentage of nitrogen (N), phosphorus (P), and potassium (K) in each mixture. For a vegetable garden, it is best to balance the numbers as evenly as possible, such as a 5-3-4 blend.

Here is how each of these ingredients works:

Nitrogen (N) is responsible for the growth of plant leaves and stems. It is beneficial for plants that are grown primarily for their foliage, such as lettuce, spinach, salad greens, kale, collard, and chard. Nitrogen is the element that is used up most quickly, and leafy plants benefit from frequent application, especially in the spring and fall. Yellowish leaves and stunted growth will indicate nitrogen deficiency. Keep the soil healthy with a cover crop such as buckwheat during the summer or winter rye grass for a fall and winter planting, which is then turned into the soil.

Phosphorus (P) is key in the development of fruit and flowers, and is especially good for the general well-being of all your plants. Adequate phosphorus in the soil is especially helpful in preventing transplant shock, and if plants show any sign of poor health, such as purple or yellow foliage, or stunted growth, it may be due to a phosphorus deficiency. Phosphorus is generally available in most soils that have been enriched with compost, but if your soil test indicates that you need more, a handful of bone meal sprinkled evenly over the garden will usually do the trick.

Potassium (K) is essential for root growth, and is especially beneficial to crops that grow primarily underground, such as carrots, beets, onions, and potatoes. A light dusting of ashes from a wood stove added to your finished compost before spreading on the garden is one of the best sources. Remember, a little bit of wood ash goes a long way, and it is easy to add too much potassium to your soil. Do not sprinkle wood ash directly over your garden or in unfinished compost—instead, add it only to your finished compost, since it will prevent the pile from heating to the high temperature necessary for breaking down other components.

Step Five: Maintenance

Weeds: When it comes to gardening, I make every effort to pull out weeds when they are still young and catch them before they go to seed. This requires a weekly regimen—and, in the height of summer, a daily routine— of plucking weeds, which have a tendency to hide under large-leaved plants. Weeds produce an enormous number of seeds, and one plant can quickly disperse baby weeds in profusion. To prevent weeds from taking over, keep the soil cultivated by gently running a hoe along the row between the plants to dislodge weed seedlings, as well as to aer- ate the soil so that it can more easily absorb water. Be sure weeds are pulled up with all the roots intact, or they will grow back. It may seem logical to add weeds to your compost pile, since what comes from the garden goes back into the garden, but resist the urge—the fertile soil of your compost pile may actu- ally encourage the weeds to take root again, unless the pile is actively hot. Instead, spread the weeds out in the hot sun for a day, forcing them to wilt completely before they are added to your pile.

Water: Thirsty plants are hungry plants; they need water in order to absorb nutrients in the soil and to maintain strong leaves and stems. Plant roots are hydrotropic, however, which means they move in the direction of water. A light sprinkling in hot weather may do more harm than good, since the roots will grow upward to reach the water. Overhead sprin- klers waste water, and may spread disease by means of the soil splashing onto the leaves. Instead, consider directing water to the roots through a soaker hose or a hose with a spigot that drips at the base of the plant, exactly where water is most needed.

Mulch: A top dressing of hay, wood chips, gravel, compost, seaweed, newspaper, or other natural material that is used primarily to retain moisture and prevent weeds from germinating is called mulch. In a vegetable garden, mulch is used selectively around plants such as tomatoes and cucumbers to keep their roots moist, or as a path material to indicate the area for walking. The type of mulch you choose will depend largely on what is available locally, but keep it as natural as possible. If you live near the sea, collect seaweed for a naturally nutrient-rich resource. Many gardeners prefer straw, since it is fairly inexpensive, biodegrades over time, and can be added to the compost pile in between layers. Mulch can also harbor leaf-eating insects, such as slugs, snails, and ear wigs, so if you notice that the leaves of your plants are vanishing, consider removing the mulch.

Step Six: Boundaries

Enclosing the perimeter of your kitchen garden with a low stone wall, a boxwood hedge, a row of espaliered fruit trees, or a rustic split-rail fence will do more than simply keep out dogs and deer. A distinctive edging creates a border, as well as a visual transition, between where the lawn ends and the garden begins. A tall wall creates privacy and can be an ideal backdrop for a trellis support, while a short wall is adequate for simply defining a separate space. Consider the type of fence or border that fits your particular garden—not only how essential it is as a barrier to rabbits and other small animals that love to visit gardens, but also how important it is to defining your own style.

Here are some popular options:

Stone Walls: There are many reasons to choose stones as the foundation for a garden bed, especially if you live in an area where these natural beauties are plentiful. Stones are durable, unique, and just plain gorgeous when combined with plants. In cooler climates, stones have the added asset of absorbing natural heat, thus providing the soil and roots with extra warmth in the early spring for a jump on the season and in the late fall to extend the season a little longer.

Picket or Split-Rail Fence: For rustic style and simplicity, consider natural wood. A wood fence provides a natural trellis for vining plants, such as pole beans, cucumbers, peas, and morning glories, to ramble upon. Also, it is easy to wrap wire within the fence to create a more secure barrier against groundhogs, rabbits, or other small animals that may visit your garden. Consider building an arbor over the gate, to create a bit of mystery within.

Evergreen or Boxwood Hedge: A tall evergreen-plant border is an option favored by anyone who appreciates classic design. Hailing back to the early monastery gardens, surrounding the garden with a year-round green hedge provides privacy as well as acts as a wind block. Evergreens enjoy a diet of high-nitrogen fertilizer; they are slow growing and easy to maintain (clipping once a year will keep their shape). Deer love to nibble on evergreens, so if you live in an area with a high deer population, consider a different choice of hedge material.

Deer Fence: Deer are a real threat to most gardeners, and the typical way to combat these intruders is to enclose the garden with an unsightly deer fence resembling a batting cage. Maybe you have tried down-home methods (that sometimes works on a small scale) of tricking deer into thinking that humans are lingering nearby: soap or hair tied to a tree, or urine-marked stones at the perimeter of the garden. Some gardeners have had luck with a fishing line or wire strung at chest level, which confuses deer by creating an invisible barrier. Whatever you choose to do, make every attempt to soften the edges of a tall deer fence with an ornamental wall of evergreens, high bush cranberries, or espaliered apple trees planted on the interior of the wall, which will also add to the ambience you are trying to create with your kitchen garden design.

Step Seven: Tools

Garden centers are like kitchen stores: They offer many more tools and gadgets than you actually need to get the job done. Some may look tempting and offer time-saving techniques, but in the end they will only create clutter in your toolshed. Plan to invest in a set of good, hard-working garden tools that you can rely on each season. Keep them organized on hooks in your toolshed or garage, and in the fall, wipe them clean, sharpen any blades, and hang the tools where they will be protected from inclement weather. Good garden tools make your job easier and will last for generations. Here's what you'll find in my garden shed:

* Garden spade
* Garden fork
* Edging tool
* Garden rake
* Scuffle hoe (two sizes: small for tight spaces, medium for keeping paths clear of weeds)
* Trowel and cultivating hand tools
* Long-handled hoe
* Dibble or planting stick
* Large ball of untreated garden twine
* Scissors and pruning shears
* Bamboo poles (various heights)
* Watering can
* Hose with adjustable nozzle
* Seed-starting trays
* Wooden stakes (to mark rows)
* Harvest baskets

A garden tool that I keep outside my shed are my honeybees. For many years, I watched honeybees from a distance until I became a "new-bee" beekeeper. I read about different types of honeybees to order, and found a beekeeping neighbor who became my mentor. The benefits go far beyond delicious honey. On sunny days, I stand close to the hive and watch the bees fly in and out, flapping their wings and spinning to indicate to other nectar gatherers how far away and in which direction a plentiful source of pollen or nectar is located. Attracting beneficial pollinators, which include moths, wasps, butterflies, birds, and toads, as well as honeybees, to your garden creates diversity and pollinates the garden. I am amazed at how much more productive my garden has become, and my neighbors are harvesting fruit from trees that have been idle for years. I check on the hives a few times during the summer to make sure they are healthy, and at the end of the season I extract honey. Build a healthy ecosystem for your garden, and enjoy the vitality that results.

Domestic honeybees are easy to set up in your backyard, and require minimum effort once they are established. Honeybees travel several miles to seek nectar from a wide variety of sources, so whether you live in the city or the country, bees will be successful. Find a local beekeeper to be your mentor and help you set up a hive.

Step Eight: Style

Invite whimsy into your garden to reflect your own personality and style. Here are a few ways to elevate your vegetable garden into a fanciful kitchen garden:

Supports and Structures: We often think of vegetables as ground-hugging plants, yet many ornamental edibles enjoy climbing, rambling, and spreading from above. Height is remarkably effective in creating drama in a kitchen garden design. Provide an assortment of trellis materials upon which pole beans, cucumbers, gourds, and tomatoes can grow, creating a wonderful vertical tapestry in the garden landscape. I use simple bamboo poles harnessed together to form a tent or teepee. Sometimes I paint them bright colors, and I often plant an assortment of annual plants to weave together, forming elaborate tunnels and tents that are especially fun in the Children's Garden. Twisty twigs tied together at the top with twine are the perfect solution for sweet peas and climbing nasturtiums.

Garden Art: There is a thin line between garden art and junk—and there is no doubt that it's a matter of personal taste. Whether you are following the latest European garden trends to discover just the right blue-green color to paint the patio furniture, or the latest on ceramic fairy houses, garden art can add fun and whimsy to your garden. If you are tempted, however, by a giant toad for the boggy end of the garden or a plastic mushroom to tuck under a hosta, remember the words of one of my favorite garden designers: "Choose objets d'art that your kids will fight over when you are gone." In other words, make it special. Gardens produce memories, and what I place in my garden is usually sentimental as well as beautiful. Search antique stores for unusual decorative garden art. A few well-placed garden goddesses are a good reminder that they are always ready to offer inspiration.

Gates: Your kitchen garden starts at the gate. A unique garden gate can suggest the style or design of the garden beyond. Maybe it's a simple wire fence, a captivating arbor smothered with climbing rose, or a welcoming wooden bench. Find something that accentuates this important transition between the lawn and the garden in a way that fits your landscape. Create a transition from the lawn into the garden with a visual cue, which may be as simple as stepping stones or a pot full of nasturtiums.

Benches: A bench in the garden does not guarantee that a gardener will sit still for a moment, but it provides the opportunity as well as a welcome reminder to take a moment to reflect and enjoy the garden. Benches can be made from stone or wood, and are best if shrouded in a shade cover of fragrant blooms.

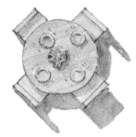

Kitchen Gardens

The Salad Lover's Garden
Greens for Health

Garden Personality: *If you crave a tidy bed of greens for an endless supply of the spicy, savory, bitter, and crisp leaves that make a truly great salad, the Salad Lover's Garden is the one for you. A series of small beds provide easy successive planting that will keep a steady supply of greens from seed to salad bowl.*

A Salad Lover's Garden can be as small as a perfect square-foot plot, or a matrix of geometric designs. For new gardeners, lettuce and salad greens are the easiest and quickest garden crops to grow and are ideal to plant in a kitchen garden. Consider a full range of European and American heirloom greens blended with gorgeous lettuces that weave together into a colorful tapestry almost too beautiful to harvest.

A garden of salad greens, either wild or cultivated, is rich in vitamins and minerals, and can contain as many as fifty different plants with flavors from buttery-soft head lettuce to piquant arugula and peppery cress. You can also grow salad onions, radishes, carrots, salad cucumbers, and a range of edible flowers to enhance the salad bowl, but in this design, salad greens steal the show with their unique blend of wild colors, textures, and shapes.

The varieties in this garden may be new to you, but they are all worth growing. Your best bet is to start with seeds, since all are easy to grow. Claytonia, which is rarely found in the farmers' market, rewards the gardener with tiny, exotic, lily pad–shaped leaves that will add an unusual visual twist to a bowl of greens. Goldgelber purslane, a cousin to the more rampant weed, is more upright, and the succulent leaves are at the top of the charts when it comes to omega-3 benefits. Mustard greens, with their sizzling hot flavor, are tamed by a good creamy dressing, especially when picked young and tender.

Start the season as early as you can work the soil, since greens enjoy the cooler weather of early spring and late fall.

Ten Tips for Growing a Salad Lover's Garden

1 Consider the benefits of raised beds to keep the beds tidy and neat. They can be as low as 6 inches or as tall as 3 feet, depending on your preference.

2 If you have a nearby hose, install a convenient drip irrigation to provide a source of water during the season, which salad greens prefer. Lettuce and salad greens are 80 percent water, so be sure to keep the plants moist.

3 Greens love cool weather, so take advantage of the spring and fall seasons to plant a crop of greens. Prepare your garden with soil that is rich in nitrogen, which feeds and supports leafy green plants. Add compost or aged manure as a good source of vitamin-rich nitrogen, and till into your soil with a garden fork before sowing seeds.

4 Most lettuce and salad greens will grow easily from seed, so plan to direct sow your seeds. Sow the seed ½ inch in the ground, tamp the soil, and mark the spot with a stick or plant tag. Plant successively every two weeks throughout the growing season.

5 Many greens are "cut-and-come-again," giving you several harvests from one sowing. Clip the leaves just above the roots. Water well, and new greens will sprout in a few weeks.

6 Combine various shapes and colors to add visual delight to a tasty salad. Plan to include spikes of color, and variegated leaves to break up the mostly green hue of the lettuce.

7 Some greens grow fast; others, such as mache, are slower to germinate, so be patient. The unique rounded, cup-shaped leaves of this mild-tasting green offer a striking contrast to a bowl of greens and are well worth the wait.

8 Flea beetles are one of the few pests that affect salad greens (other than rabbits) and they can leave your greens with small holes. To prevent flea beetle damage, cover your greens immediately with a floating row cover after planting.

9 At the end of the season, plant a cover crop of buckwheat or annual rye grass to keep building the nitrogen in your soil, essential for healthy greens.

10 Harvest salad greens with scissors, just above the root line. For clean greens, harvest before a rainstorm to prevent splatter from soil. A salad spinner makes washing and drying greens easy; then wrap the washed greens in a paper towel prior to serving to absorb excess moisture.

OVERALL SIZE: *15 feet by 15 feet*
BED SIZE: *(4) 6-foot triangles*
PATH WIDTH: *3 feet*
FENCING: *Wattle or raised bed*
PATH MATERIAL: *Pea stone gravel or grass*

Salad Lover's Garden Plant List

1 Arugula

2 Basil: Sweet Genovese,
Red Rubin, and Lemon

3 Chervil

4 Claytonia

5 Cress

6 Lettuce: Looseleaf Mix and
Mixed Head

7 Mache: Vit or Piedmont

8 Mesclun Mixes: Misticanza,
Provencal, and Nicoise

9 Purslane: Goldgelber

10 Radicchio

11 Sorrel

12 Spinach

13 Nasturtium

 Arugula

This piquant, peppery salad green is a star in most mesclun mixes, and will grow rapidly. For best flavor, pick the leaves young, since the summer heat will add a hot flavor, and water frequently to keep the plant from going to seed. Direct sow seeds in the garden in prepared loose soil. Seeds can be planted tightly in a single row or broadcast in a block; allow 5 inches between rows in order to cultivate. Keep plants watered and harvest with scissors when 3 to 5 inches tall. Arugula is a cut-and-come-again crop, but the stems become woody as the season progresses, so plan to allow it to grow only once again before reseeding. Favorites: Sylvetta, Astro.

7 Mache

This once wild green has unique rounded, cup-shaped leaves; these sweet rosettes call for little more than a simple dressing of walnut oil and sherry vinegar or a twist of lemon to balance their mild, nutty flavor. Cold tolerant and compact, this delicate green is best served on its own or in the classic Swiss recipe with chopped beets and croutons. Direct sow seeds in the garden in prepared loose soil. Seeds can be planted tightly in a single row or broadcast in a block; allow 5 inches between rows in order to cultivate. Keep plants watered and harvest with scissors when small rosettes are formed, about 3 inches tall.

⑧ Mesclun

Mesclun makes it easy for salad lovers to harvest a range of greens from a single packet of seeds. Based on a blend of greens, mesclun can be grown with as much success in a window box as in the garden. Individual components of mesclun can be planted separately, and then combined together in the salad bowl. Direct sow seeds in the garden in prepared loose soil. Seeds can be planted tightly in a single row or broadcast in a block; allow 5 inches between rows in order to cultivate. Keep plants watered and harvest with scissors when 5 to 8 inches tall. For a cut-and-come-again crop, leave roots in the ground, and another crop will resprout. Favorites: Provencal, Misticanza, Nicoise.

⑩ Radicchio

Italian chicory was once difficult to grow, but newer varieties develop heads of crimson-red leaves in a single season. Direct sow seeds in the garden in prepared loose soil or start in plug trays and transplant. Keep plants watered and harvest when tight heads form, about 5 inches across in about 60 days from sowing. Favorites: Chioggia, Indigo, Fiero.

⑪ Sorrel

Faithful sorrel is worth its weight in gold. It is a hardy perennial green that shoots out an abundance of long, arrow-shaped leaves that are tart and ascorbic.

Arugula and Mint Thai Soup

Quick and light, this soup is simple to make and simply delicious. The recipe is for four servings, but you will easily see how the ingredients can be adjusted to turn into a fast lunch for one. The lemon and garlic add zing that can be intensified with a splash of hot sauce or a grating of fresh ginger. *Serves 4*

1 cup Jasmine rice

Zest and juice of 1 lemon

4 ounces fresh crabmeat

1 cup arugula (or watercress), torn into bite-size pieces

1 medium carrot, finely shredded (about 1 cup)

6 spring radishes, julienned

2 scallions, finely chopped

4 cups vegetable stock, heated to a simmer

8 spearmint leaves, cut into chiffonade

Lemon gem marigolds, for garnish

1 Fill four soup bowls with boiling water to heat and set aside.

2 In a saucepan over medium heat, simmer Jasmine rice with 2 cups of water and cook until water is absorbed, about 20 minutes. Toss the rice with the lemon zest and stir in the lemon juice. Set aside.

3 Meanwhile, simmer the crabmeat in boiling water to cover until just tender, about 5 minutes. Drain and break into bite-size chunks.

4 When ready to serve, pour the water from the soup bowls. Place a mound of the rice in each bowl and add equal quantities of crabmeat, arugula, carrots, radishes, and scallions.

5 Ladle the stock into each bowl, and add the spearmint leaves. Garnish with a single lemon gem marigold and serve immediately.

Grilled Romaine and Radicchio with Honey Blue Cheese Dressing

In Italy, all head chicories are called radicchio, named after the region in which they originated. In America, the term is applied only to the red varieties, and I prefer to grow the exotically beautiful Treviso radicchio. Shaped like a slender romaine lettuce, Treviso has deep burgundy leaves and white central stems. The assertive dressing offsets the smoky greens in a flamboyant way.

Serves 4

2 large heads romaine

2 heads radicchio, preferably Treviso

2 tablespoons extra virgin olive oil,
  plus extra for brushing greens

Salt and freshly ground pepper, to taste

½ cup crumbled blue cheese

1 tablespoon balsamic vinegar

3 tablespoons heavy cream

1 tablespoon honey

1 teaspoon finely chopped fresh thyme

⅓ cup chopped walnuts or pine nuts, dry
  roasted

1 Build a charcoal fire in an outdoor grill and let it burn until the coals are covered with white ash. Let the fire burn down to medium-hot (you should be able to hold your hand over the grill and leave it for about 3 seconds). For a gas grill, preheat on high, then lower to medium.

2 Cut each head of romaine and radicchio into quarters lengthwise, through the stem. Brush the wedges with oil and season with salt and pepper. Grill with the smooth outer side of the head facing down over the coals, until the leaves are charred but the head is still tender, about 10 minutes. (Round radicchio may take longer than the thinner Treviso.) Cut the radicchio and the romaine, including the charred leaves, into thin strips. Transfer to a large salad bowl.

3 In a small bowl, mash the blue cheese with a fork and gradually work in the vinegar, heavy cream, honey, and thyme. Pour over the greens, and garnish with the nuts and toss. Serve warm.

Mache and Chicken Salad with Lemon Tahini Dressing

Mache is a delicate, spoon-shaped green that deserves a light, fruity dressing to complement its natural qualities. In this salad, the flavors of spring are showcased with new red-skinned potatoes, lemon tahini dressing, and sautéed chicken. *Serves 4 to 6*

1 pound new or baby red potatoes (about 8)

1 pound chicken tenders

¼ teaspoon salt

¼ teaspoon freshly ground pepper

1 tablespoon extra virgin olive oil

½ clove garlic

Salt, to taste

4 cups mache

½ cup Lemon Tahini Dressing (see page 51)

1 cup shelled English peas (about 1½ pounds unshelled), blanched

1 tablespoon finely chopped shallot

1 Place a steamer basket in a large saucepan, add 2 inches of water, and bring to a boil. Put the potatoes in the basket and steam until barely tender when pierced with a sharp knife, 15–20 minutes, depending on size. When the potatoes are cool enough to handle, slice or quarter them.

2 Toss the chicken with ¼ teaspoon each of salt and pepper. Heat the oil in a large nonstick skillet over medium heat. Add the chicken and cook until golden brown and cooked through, about 4 minutes per side. Transfer to a clean cutting board to cool. Shred into bite-size pieces.

3 Season a wooden salad bowl by rubbing with the garlic and a pinch of salt. Chop the garlic and add to the bowl along with the potatoes and mache. Pour the dressing over the potatoes and greens; gently toss to coat. Add the peas, shallot, and shredded chicken; toss gently and serve.

Dandelion Tortellini Salad with Creamy Tomato Dressing

Cultivated dandelion greens are milder than their wild cousins, but adding a bit of bacon and cheese here will tame the bite. In this main-dish salad, a classic BLT combination is recreated with a new twist. *Serves 4*

1 pound cheese tortellini

Salt, to taste, for boiling

2 pieces thick bacon

1 tablespoon olive oil

1 sweet red onion, chopped

1 pound (about 4 cups) dandelion leaves, washed, dried, and finely chopped

1 tablespoon red wine vinegar

¼ cup Creamy Tomato Dressing (see page 49)

¼ cup Parmigiano-Reggiano cheese, grated

1 Drop the tortellini into a kettle of salted boiling water. Cover and cook until tender, about 8 minutes. Drain and set aside.

2 In a skillet over medium heat, cook the bacon until crisp. Transfer to a paper towel to drain, and pour out most of the rendered fat, reserving about 1 tablespoon.

3 Add the oil to the skillet and sauté the onion until soft, about 5 minutes. Add the dandelion leaves to the skillet and cook until wilted, about 5 minutes. Pour in the vinegar to deglaze the pan, scraping up the bits of bacon from the sides.

4 Add the cooked tortellini and toss to distribute evenly with the greens. Transfer to four pasta bowls and toss with the dressing to taste. Sprinkle with crumbled bacon and the cheese and serve.

Insalata di Misticanza with Coriander-Spiked Salmon

This piquant salad of fresh, wild greens and herbs can include up to 15 different ingredients, including a blend of colorful lettuce and chicory accented by light herbs such as borage and mint. The exact combination will depend entirely on what is available in your own garden, but here is the basis for a classic early-spring salad topped with a sweet dressing and spicy grilled salmon.

Serves 4

1 clove garlic

6 cups mixed mesclun greens (cutting lettuce, arugula, mache, radicchio, young spinach, purslane, curly endive, mint, dandelion, and sorrel), washed, dried, and torn into bite-size pieces

¼ cup finely chopped Italian flat-leaf parsley

1 small fennel bulb, trimmed, fronds removed, and finely chopped

1 small sweet red onion

2 tablespoons ground coriander seeds

1½ pounds wild salmon fillet, skinned and cut into 4 even pieces

Salt and pepper, to taste

2 tablespoons olive oil

¼ cup Maple Balsamic Vinaigrette (see facing page)

1 lemon, cut into wedges

Edible flowers, for garnish

1 Season a large wooden salad bowl by rubbing it with the garlic and a pinch of salt. Place the greens in the prepared bowl and add the parsley, fennel, and onion; toss to combine.

2 Dry roast the coriander seeds in a skillet until golden and fragrant. Cool slightly, and crush with a mortar and pestle until a fine dust.

3 Season the salmon on both sides with the coriander seeds, salt, and pepper. Heat the oil in a cast-iron skillet over high heat. Sear the salmon for about 4 minutes on each side, and remove from the heat.

4 Dress the greens with the vinaigrette to taste, and divide onto four plates. Top each with a piece of grilled salmon and a lemon wedge. Garnish with edible flowers and serve.

Maple Balsamic Vinaigrette

Here is a robust dressing that is both sweet and savory, yet allows the flavors of greens to shine through—it will quickly become a favorite for all your mesclun salads.

Makes ½ cup

1 teaspoon Dijon mustard

1 large clove garlic, finely chopped

2 tablespoons pure maple syrup

1 tablespoon lemon juice

3 tablespoons balsamic vinegar

1 tablespoon finely chopped fresh basil

½ cup extra virgin olive oil

Coarse sea salt and fresh ground pepper, to taste

In a small bowl or a blender, combine the mustard, garlic, maple syrup, lemon juice, vinegar, and basil. Slowly whisk in the olive oil to emulsify. Season to taste with salt and pepper. Transfer to a jar and store in the refrigerator for up to one week.

Creamy Tomato Dressing

With its dazzling red color and creamy texture, this dressing will quickly become a favorite for a variety of greens and cooked vegetables, or as a dipping sauce for crudités.

Makes 1 cup

2 ounces goat cheese (about ¼ cup)

2 tablespoons tarragon vinegar

2 teaspoons maple syrup

2 ripe medium tomatoes, coarsely chopped (about 2 cups)

¼ cup extra virgin olive oil

Coarse sea salt and freshly ground pepper, to taste

In a blender or food processor, combine the cheese, vinegar, and maple syrup and purée. With the motor running, add the tomatoes and the oil until the mixture is smooth. Season with salt and pepper, and transfer to a bowl or 1-pint Mason jar with a lid until ready to use.

Crispy Sorrel-and-Spinach Tartlets

This is a dressed-up version of Greek spanakopita; frilly layers of phyllo dough surround the festive spinach, sorrel, and sun-dried tomato filling. Serve these as a main dish for supper and you're sure to please vegetarians and omnivores alike. This dish can be made in a round or rectangular tart pan, but I prefer smaller tartlet pans for individual servings. *Makes 8 tartlets*

6 cups fresh spinach, washed and de-stemmed

2 cups fresh sorrel

6 tablespoons olive oil, divided

1 small yellow onion, peeled and coarsely chopped

2 eggs

½ cup ricotta cheese

½ cup feta or 4 ounces goat cheese

1 tablespoon fresh or 1 teaspoon dried dill

⅛ teaspoon grated nutmeg

¼ cup sun-dried tomatoes, reconstituted for 10 minutes in boiling water

½ teaspoon salt

¼ teaspoon freshly ground pepper

4 tablespoons (½ stick) unsalted butter

½ package phyllo dough, defrosted according to package directions

1 Fill a one-quart saucepan with water and bring to a boil. Add the spinach and sorrel and simmer until wilted, about 2 minutes. Transfer to a colander to drain and run under cool water to stop the cooking. Squeeze gently between your hands to remove the excess water and coarsely chop.

2 Heat 2 tablespoons of the olive oil in a sauté pan over medium heat and brown the onion until tender, about 5 minutes. Add the chopped spinach and sorrel to the pan and sauté for another 5 minutes. Season lightly with salt and pepper.

3 In a large bowl or food processor, whip together the eggs, cheeses, dill, and nutmeg. Finely chop the sun-dried tomatoes and add them to the cheese mixture. Fold in the sautéed sorrel, spinach, and onion.

4 Preheat the oven to 350°F. In a small saucepan, melt the butter with the remaining 4 tablespoons olive oil.

5 Remove the phyllo from the package and set it out on the counter, near the melted butter and oil. With a pastry brush, paint the insides of eight tartlet pans with the melted butter-oil mixture.

6 Place one sheet of phyllo dough inside a pan, pressing it into the edges. Fold it over to create two layers and brush with butter again. (Note: Phyllo comes in different sizes, but it will generally be large enough to fold in half to create two layers from one sheet.) Continue adding sheets and painting with the butter-oil mixture until you have eight layers. Repeat this method for each of the eight tartlet pans.

7 Fill each of the tartlet pans evenly with the sorrel-and-spinach filling. With a rolling pin or the back of a spoon, press down on the edges of the pan to trim off the excess phyllo dough, exposing the center of the filling.

8 Place the tartlet pans on a baking sheet and bake for 25 minutes. Remove from the oven and cool slightly. To remove the tartlets from their pans, run a butter knife around the edges and shake the tartlets onto a rack. Serve warm.

Lemon Tahini Dressing

Extra virgin olive oil and lemon juice are the backbone of this dressing, but it gets a unique boost from tahini, a thick paste of ground sesame seeds. Look for it in large supermarkets in the Middle Eastern section or near other nut butters. This healthy dressing is a perfect pairing for a wide range of tender spring greens.   *Makes 1¼ cups*

½ cup lemon juice

⅓ cup extra virgin olive oil

⅓ cup tahini

2 tablespoons honey

2 cloves garlic, minced

1 teaspoon salt

Freshly ground pepper, to taste

Combine the lemon juice, oil, tahini, honey, and garlic in a blender, a jar with a tight-fitting lid, or a medium bowl. Blend, shake, or whisk until smooth. Season with the salt and pepper.

Salad Greens

Bottled dressing is not an option in my kitchen. I serve green salad for dinner every night, tossed in a wooden salad bowl with a light vinaigrette. My recipe follows the classic proportions I learned from my grandmother: three parts oil, one part vinegar. But after that, the recipe gets loose, depending on the type of lettuce and the piquancy of the greens. If the leaves are soft and buttery, I'll use lemon instead of vinegar to mix with the olive oil. A tough romaine deserves bold balsamic vinegar and often a teaspoon of Dijon mustard, and a spicy salad takes a splash of maple syrup. Homegrown greens deserve homemade dressing, so keep it simple and match the greens to the dressing, rather than the other way around.

The Organic Rotation Garden
Four-Square Principles

Garden Personality: *This design is ideal for first-time gardeners with the goal of learning the fundamental principles of organic gardening. The four-square design is one of the oldest and most practical designs, and it provides the building block for many of the other garden designs in this book.*

The history of the four-square garden goes back seven centuries, to the first English cottage gardens, when the landholding aristocracy offered four-square parcels of land to the working class, who had been decimated by the plague during the thirteenth century. In these four-square gardens, they could grow food for their families, as well as supply the upper class with grains, herbs, berries, fruit, and livestock. This practical and productive four-square design continued to evolve through the centuries, then flourished when more aesthetic elements were introduced, such as espaliered trees, ornamental flowers, and fragrant herbs.

When you combine this classic design with the principles of organic gardening, you will appreciate how the basics of organic rotation work, making it easy to follow a successful planting routine each year. The end result will be healthy soil, healthy plants, and a harvest that is vitamin-rich and packed with flavor.

When plants are grown in the same location year after year, they can be weakened by soil-borne diseases. This may lead to weakened (or dead) plants, and may tempt you to find a short-term chemical solution to keep the plants alive. In the Organic Rotation Garden, you are creating a garden that will be self-sustaining as well as self-improving every year. You are working with nature to constantly upgrade the natural balance in your vegetable garden.

A four-square Organic Rotation Garden simplifies the process of figuring out where to place your plants every year, because once you learn the basic premise of rotation, you will enjoy a more bountiful garden.

Ten Tips for Growing an Organic Rotation Garden

1 The four equal squares constitute an easy garden design to carve into existing lawn. If you would prefer to create raised beds instead, be sure to select untreated wood and bury the boards partially into the ground for stability.

2 Mark the beds with a waterproof marker and a stake, noting which bed is designated for the specific crop rotation: nitrogen (N), phosphorus (P), potassium (K), and builders (B). At the end of the season, you will rotate the stakes in the beds clockwise, and repeat this each year.

3 Group your seeds and plants according to the above system. Predetermine which plants will be direct sown into the garden and which will be started in a plug tray or purchased and transplanted into the garden.

4 Select annual flowers for the central beds that will attract beneficial insects and pollinate the flowers of your vegetables and fruits.

5 Set up tomato teepees and other structures before the plants get too big, and allow plenty of space in between the plants for healthy growth. An overcrowded garden can all too quickly become a jumble of plants and diminish the harvest.

6 Set down stepping-stones or boards within the garden beds to lessen soil compaction around the growing areas.

7 Weeds will rob your soil of nutrients, so keep the soil cultivated and weed free.

8 At the end of the season, apply a layer of compost or well-aged manure, and then plant a cover crop to aid in the nutrition of the soil and to enhance stability, to prevent the soil from washing away during winter snow or rain.

9 Consider keeping a garden journal to track the progress of your garden throughout the season. Take time to observe how the beneficial pollinators gather on the annual flowers, and notice how your plants adapt to soil improvements and the changes in the weather. Build a foundation of garden techniques that lead to a healthy practice.

10 Seal your unused seed packets and store them in a dry, cool location until the following season. Be sure the year that they were purchased is clearly marked. Many seeds will last for several years, while some varieties are only viable for one season.

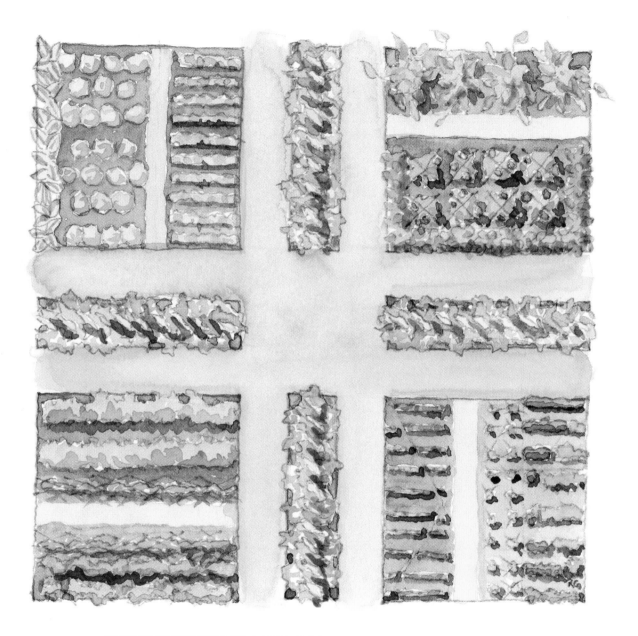

OVERALL SIZE: *26 feet by 26 feet*
BED SIZE: *10 feet by 10 feet*
PATH WIDTH: *4 feet*
PERIMETER FLOWER BORDER: *2 feet*
RAISED BED: *Cedar*
PATH MATERIAL: *Bark mulch*

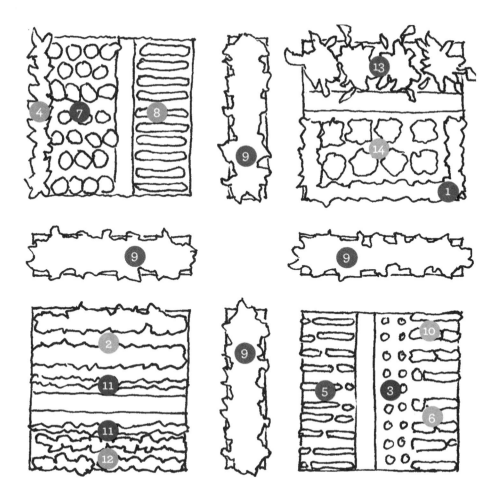

Organic Rotation Garden Plant List

1. Basil: Sweet Genovese

2. Bush Beans: Provider (green), Rocdor (yellow), and Royal Burgundy (purple)

3. Carrots: Mokum

4. Chard: Rainbow

5. Garlic: Spanish Roja

6. Leeks: Upton (early) and Striker (late)

7. Lettuce: Mixed Butterheads

8. Mesclun Greens: Misticanza, Provencal, and Nicoise

9. Mixed Annual Flowers: Valentine Sunflowers, Calendula, Snapdragon, and Zinnia

10. Onions: Candy

11. Peas: Organ Giant

12. Potatoes

13. Squash: Summer Multipik (yellow) and Elite (green)

14. Tomatoes: Garden Peach, Persimmon, and Green Zebra

② Beans

Sometimes gardening requires making tough choices—when it comes to planting pole beans or bush beans, I vote in favor of both! Plant pole beans on a trellis and you will find that the succulent beans are easy to spot and to harvest without bending down. Bush beans are tidy, compact plants. Before sowing bean seed, roll the seeds in inoculants, which will trigger the nitrogen and increase your luscious yields. (These are available through garden centers or seed catalogs.) Sow one seed about 1 inch deep, planting every 5 inches in a row or at the base of a trellis. Water, and seedlings should emerge within five to seven days. Flowers will appear, and beans will follow. Pole bean favorites: Trionfo Violetto Purple, Kwintus, Blauhilde, Borlotti. Bush bean favorites: Fin de Bagnols, Nickel, Royal Burgundy, Roc d'Or, Blue Lake.

③ Carrot

Carrots are a mainstay of the kitchen garden, and for good reason. Plucking a deep-orange carrot from the ground is one of the great pleasures of summertime. Carrots are readily available at farmers' markets, so it pays to do your research and plant unusual varieties that are bred for their remarkable flavor. Carrots are best grown in light, aerated soil; if your soil is mostly clay, plan to grow the shorter, baby type that need less depth to develop full flavor. Carrots are members of the Umbelliferae family, which comprises dill and about three thousand other species, including many spices containing medicinal properties. Direct sow seeds in the garden; they can take up to two weeks to emerge, which is why I recommend combining them with radish seeds to break the soil. Plan to thin carrots several times before harvesting to give them plenty of room to grow to the desired width as well as depth. Favorites: Touchon, Napoli, Minicor, Thumbelina.

4 Chard

One of the best ornamental garden plants for kitchen gardeners, the long-season chard is equally useful as a decorative border plant and as a valuable source of mineral-rich greens for the cook. Direct sow seeds in the garden in prepared loose soil or prestart in plug trays and transplant. Keep plants watered, and once the plant has established an upright form, harvest the outer leaves as needed. Keep roots intact, and leaves will continue to resprout for a long season of growth. Favorites: Bright Lights, Rainbow, Charlotte, Virgo.

13 Summer Squash

Summer squash is so easy to find in the markets that I am reluctant to give it space in a kitchen garden. But for those who can't get enough of it, I recommend that you place them on the edge of your garden to allow their wide girth to spread. Start seeds indoors and transplant, or direct sow in the garden. Favorites: Gadzukes, Tromboncino, Sunburst, Ronde de Nice.

Summer Squash Soup with Mint Pistou

Gardeners can't resist growing squash, and with good reason—they are as versatile as can be. From soups to entrées, from side dishes to cakes, you always can find a way to use up that surplus zucchini or yellow squash. It's hard to believe there is no cream in this soup, and the swirl of minty pistou adds to its complexity.   *Serves 6*

2 tablespoons unsalted butter

1 large onion, chopped

2 cloves garlic

1 tablespoon curry powder

1 teaspoon ground ginger

½ teaspoon turmeric

3 medium summer squash, trimmed and coarsely chopped (about 4 cups)

4 small red-skinned potatoes, peeled

6 cups water

½ cup canned unsweetened coconut milk, to taste

Salt and freshly ground pepper, to taste

Parsley Mint Pistou (see page 65), for garnish

1 Heat the butter in a large pot over medium heat. Add the onion and garlic and cook, stirring occasionally, until the onion is softened, about 5 minutes. Add the curry powder, ginger, and turmeric and stir until very fragrant, about 30 seconds.

2 Add the squash and potatoes and cover. Cook, stirring often, until they begin to soften, about 5 minutes. Add the water and bring to a boil. Reduce the heat to medium-low and cover. Simmer until the vegetables are tender, about 30 minutes.

3 With an immersion blender, purée the soup, adding just enough coconut milk to reach the desired consistency and flavor. Season lightly with salt and pepper. Cover and refrigerate until chilled, at least 2 hours. To serve, swirl 1 tablespoon pistou into each bowl of soup.

Carrot and Tarragon Tart

When carrots are in season, they can be used in soups and stews, but I prefer to bake them in this savory tart. You'll love the easy dough recipe, which is wonderfully pliable and can be rolled out right away or chilled for later. Season it with herbs to perfume the kitchen with a sweet aroma as it bakes. *Makes one 9-inch tart or pie (8 servings)*

DOUGH

1 cup unbleached white flour

½ cup whole-wheat flour

1 tablespoon fresh tarragon

½ teaspoon salt

8 tablespoons (1 stick) unsalted butter, chilled and cut into 1-inch cubes

½ cup plain yogurt

FILLING

2 tablespoons extra virgin olive oil

1 sweet red onion, thinly sliced

1½ cups grated carrots

1 tablespoon Dijon mustard

½ cup grated Vermont cheddar cheese

1 cup half-and-half

2 large eggs

1 tablespoon finely chopped fresh tarragon

¼ teaspoon salt

½ teaspoon freshly ground pepper

1 Preheat the oven to 350°F.

2 Prepare the crust: In the bowl of a food processor, combine the flours, tarragon, and salt and pulse to blend. With the motor running, add the butter, one piece at a time, until incorporated. Add the yogurt and pulse just until the dough starts to come together.

3 Transfer the dough to a lightly floured surface, press into a ball, and press flat with the palm of your hand. Using a floured rolling pin, gently roll into a 10-inch circle and transfer to a tart pan or shallow pie dish. Bake the crust until set but not browned, about 15 minutes. Let cool on a wire rack.

4 Prepare the filling: Heat the oil in a large skillet over medium heat. Add the onions and cook, stirring, until tender and golden, about 5 minutes.

5 Drop the carrots into a saucepan of salted boiling water and cook for 3 minutes. Drain and add to the onions and cook, stirring, for 2 minutes. Remove from the heat.

6 Brush the mustard over the baked crust, sprinkle with the cheese, then spread the carrot mixture evenly into the tart shell.

7 In a small bowl or measuring cup, whisk together the half-and-half, eggs, tarragon, and the salt and pepper. Place the tart shell on a baking tray, and pour the yogurt filling over the carrot mixture in the shell.

8 Bake the tart until the filling is firm and the edges are golden, 35–40 minutes. Cool slightly before slicing. Serve warm or chilled.

Warm Winter Salad with Roasted Garlic Dressing

The sweetness of roasted garlic vinaigrette served warm over spinach tenderizes the leaves and creates a perfect melt-in-your-mouth salad. The colorful carrot and cabbage add a healthful crunch, and the flavors blend beautifully. *Serves 4*

½ cup pine nuts

1 recipe Roasted Garlic Dressing
  (see page 65)

1 shallot, finely chopped (2 tablespoons)

4 cups spinach, washed and rinsed,
  stems removed

1 cup grated carrots

2 cups grated cabbage

½ cup dried cranberries

4 ounces plain chèvre (soft goat cheese),
  crumbled

Salt and freshly ground pepper, to taste

1 In a skillet over medium heat, dry roast the pine nuts until golden brown, about 3 minutes. While they toast, make your dressing. Transfer to a small bowl.

2 Return the saucepan to the heat, and gently heat the dressing. Add the shallots and simmer for 3–5 minutes, until soft.

3 Meanwhile, tear the spinach into bite-size pieces. In a large bowl, combine the spinach with the carrots and cabbage. Pour the hot dressing over the greens, carrots, and cabbage and toss to coat. Allow to marinate for about 5 minutes, until softened. Sprinkle with the pine nuts, dried cranberries, and chèvre. Season with salt and pepper and serve.

Lettuce and Mesclun with Herbed Vinaigrette

Bottled dressing is not an option in my kitchen. Instead, I make this easy vinaigrette to complement delicate-flavored lettuce and mesclun greens. The quality of the ingredients directly affects the outcome, however, and while good-quality extra virgin olive oil is accessible, selecting the right vinegar is a challenge. I prefer to make my own herbed vinegar, then mix and match to balance the greens in the bowl. *Serves 4*

1 clove garlic

¼ teaspoon coarse sea salt

4 tablespoons red wine vinegar

1 heaping teaspoon Dijon mustard

1 heaping teaspoon honey

1 teaspoon finely chopped fresh chervil

1 teaspoon finely chopped fresh basil

¼ cup extra virgin olive oil

Freshly ground pepper, to taste

4 cups mixed lettuce leaves

2 cups mesclun leaves

1 lemon

1 Season a wooden salad bowl by rubbing the garlic clove inside the bowl and sprinkling with the salt. Remove the garlic clove, finely chop, and place back in the bowl, along with the vinegar.

2 Add the mustard, honey, chervil, and basil. Slowly pour in the olive oil and whisk with a spoon until emulsified. Season with pepper.

3 Wash and dry the greens, tear them into bite-size pieces, and add them to the salad bowl. When ready to serve, toss with the dressing from the bottom of the bowl, until completely coated. Squeeze the lemon on top and toss once more.

Wilted Chard with Ginger-Lime Tuna Steaks

By fall, chard is abundant and you'll be searching for ways to prepare it. Try this recipe for spicy marinated tuna layered on a bed of wilted chard. You can grill it outside, or under the broiler for a quick preparation. In order to bring everything to the table hot, plan to marinate the fish while you prepare the chard and vinaigrette.   *Serves 4*

½ teaspoon salt

¼ teaspoon freshly ground pepper

1 teaspoon grated fresh ginger

1 tablespoon finely chopped fresh thyme

2 tablespoons tamari sauce

1 tablespoon fresh lemon juice

2 tablespoons olive oil

4 tuna steaks, each about 1 inch thick
  (2 pounds total)

12 large rainbow chard leaves with stems

½ cup Ginger-Lime Vinaigrette
  (see facing page), to taste

Fresh Italian flat-leaf parsley, for garnish

1 In a shallow baking pan, blend together the salt, pepper, ginger, thyme, tamari, lemon juice, and olive oil. Place the tuna steaks in the marinade, brushing both sides. Cover with plastic wrap and let stand for 1 hour.

2 Meanwhile, prepare the chard: Trim the leaves from the stems. Coarsely chop the leaves and the stems and drop them into a pot of boiling salted water. Cover and cook until wilted, about 4 minutes. Drain and toss with the vinaigrette dressing, reserving several tablespoons for final plating.

3 Preheat the broiler. Arrange the steaks in an ovenproof baking pan and place under the broiler, about 4 inches from the source of heat. Broil for 5 minutes, leaving the oven door partly open. Turn the steaks over and broil for another 5 minutes. Remove from the oven and cut inside to check for doneness. The center should remain pink.

4 Place a layer of the chard on a warm plate, top with a piece of broiled tuna, and spoon another drizzle of the vinaigrette over the tuna. Garnish with the parsley and serve.

Parsley Mint Pistou   *Makes ½ cup*

¼ cup loosely packed fresh mint leaves

½ cup loosely packed fresh Italian flat-leaf parsley

2 scallions, chopped (about ¼ cup)

¼ cup extra virgin olive oil

2 tablespoons water

½ teaspoon salt

Place the herbs and scallions in the bowl of a food processor and pulse until finely chopped. With the motor running, add the oil in a stream, then add the water and salt, blending until smooth. Store in a jar until you are ready to use.

Roasted Garlic Dressing   *Makes ½ cup*

2 heads garlic

½ cup olive oil, plus 1 tablespoon for drizzling

3 tablespoons balsamic vinegar

Juice of 1 lime

Salt and freshly ground pepper, to taste

1 Preheat the oven to 400°F. Without peeling the garlic heads, drizzle them with 1 tablespoon olive oil, wrap them in foil, and place them on a baking dish in the middle rack of the oven. Bake for 35 minutes, or until the cloves are tender to the pinch.

2 Unwrap the foil and let the garlic sit until just cool enough to handle. Using kitchen shears, snip off the pointed tops of the garlic heads, hold upside down over a bowl, and gently squeeze the garlic so that the soft pulp falls into the bowl.

3 Blend in the remaining ingredients and stir until smooth.

Ginger-Lime Vinaigrette   *Makes ½ cup*

1 tablespoon tamari

2 cloves garlic, chopped

1 (1-inch) knob fresh ginger, peeled and grated (2 teaspoons)

¼ cup rice wine vinegar

½ cup extra virgin olive oil

2 tablespoons finely chopped fresh cilantro

Juice of 2 limes

Combine all the ingredients in a blender. Whir for 10 seconds.

The Cook's Garden
A Classic *Potager*

Garden Personality: *This classic garden is planted with the cook in mind, with ample amounts of tender greens and aromatic herbs conveniently located near the kitchen door. During the summer, this garden becomes an extension of your kitchen.*

The word "garden" derives from an old German word, *gart*, which means enclosure or safe place. This classic garden design is based on my own *potager* (the French term for "kitchen garden"), which fits snugly against the south side of my house, on less than a quarter of an acre. Surrounded by emerald green arborvitae, which frame the front and side border, the hedge provides privacy from neighbors. Boundaries around your garden may not seem like a priority at first, but they create a transition between the lawn and the garden. Stepping inside the garden feels private, and the space feels as cozy as a small room.

A Cook's Garden is a classic *potager*, designed to grow those tender greens and aromatic herbs that are used by the cook on a daily basis. Gardeners have intermingled vegetables, fruits, flowers, and herbs since medieval times, and for the French, the *potager* continues to be an integral part of their lifestyle. More than 25 percent of the fruit and vegetables consumed by the French are homegrown, which explains why the French are known for their enjoyment of cooking and consuming good food.

A Cook's Garden is compact and efficient, with sufficient space for a dozen or more different salad greens and herbs, a few heirloom tomatoes, edible flowers, and delicate plants that are only available from your own kitchen garden. Select seeds for unusual varieties that pique your interest, and experiment with a range of flavors that are unfamiliar but will spark you to try new recipes.

Ten Tips for Growing a Cook's Garden

1 Situate the garden where you can see it from inside the house. Try to create a view from a window and look closely at how the plan fits into your surrounding landscape.

2 Think about convenience: Is there a nearby garden faucet? Will the garden need protection from the wind? Is there a tree that is blocking available summer sun?

3 Create boundaries with a hedge or a fence early in the process. Think of it as part of the garden design, rather than as an afterthought.

4 Include vertical accents and focal points, as you would a perennial flower bed. These can be temporary, such as a tomato tower, bean teepee, or sweet-pea trellis.

5 Be creative when you plant, to add interest and whimsy. Think beyond straight rows, to how you can sow seeds in spiral, arched, checkerboard, or wagon-wheel patterns.

6 Edge each of the garden beds with an annual flower to provide a splash of color and a unified look. Annual flowers also help mask bare spots as the season progresses and vegetable crops are harvested.

7 Keep fast-growing plants—such as head lettuce, chervil, mustard, and mesclun—growing from early spring to late fall. Plant successively every two weeks throughout the season.

8 Plant night-blooming flowers and fragrant herbs along the edges, to enhance the evening romance of the kitchen garden.

9 Don't be tricked by the diminutive size of the seedlings. By midsummer, the garden will fill out, so be sure to allow plenty of space for each plant to grow.

10 Once a crop is done, plant another. Keep planting the short-season crops that will provide a second yield. Keep the soil in use, to prevent weeds from germinating and robbing the soil of nutrients.

OVERALL SIZE: *48 feet by 48 feet*
ACTUAL VEGETABLE GARDEN SIZE: *40 feet by 40 feet*
BED SIZE: *10 feet by 10 feet / CUT OUT AT CENTER / DEPTH: 2 feet*
CENTER BED: *4 feet*
PATH WIDTH: *4 feet / CENTRAL PATH: 2½ feet*
MIXED BORDER: *4 feet wide / Arborvitae, boxwood, and peonies*
PATH MATERIAL: *Bark mulch*

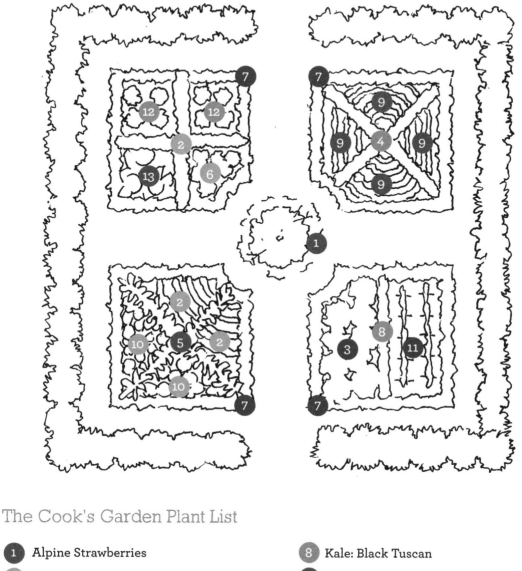

The Cook's Garden Plant List

1 Alpine Strawberries

2 Basil: Sweet Genovese and Mammoth Leaf

3 Beans: Trionfo Violetto

4 Beets: Perpetual Spinach

5 Chard: Rainbow

6 Cucumbers

7 Edible Flowers: Nasturtiums,
   Gem Marigolds, and Alyssum

8 Kale: Black Tuscan

9 Mesclun: Mixed Greens

10 Mixed Herbs: Chives, Parsley, Tarragon,
   Summer Savory, Marjoram, Rosemary,
   Dill, and Thyme

11 Peas: Sugar Snap

12 Peppers: Cayenne Hot

13 Tomatoes: Green Zebra, Sun Gold,
   Persimmon, and Big Rainbow

① Alpine Strawberries

There are close to a hundred varieties of Alpine strawberries, yet many are not readily available to the home gardener. Plants can be grown from seed, or propagated from cuttings. Alpine strawberries are best planted in the early spring, in full or part sun, requiring only six hours of intense sun in order to fruit. This makes them especially good around the base of fruit trees, or bordering the edge of a kitchen garden. Some species of Alpine strawberries will send out runners; these can be trimmed regularly to keep the plants vigorous.

⑩ Mixed Herbs

Selecting herbs for your kitchen garden will fall into two general categories: annuals and perennials. A typical herb garden will contain a mixture of both. Perennial herbs offer year-round growth, although in the winter they will go dormant. Welcome both into your herb garden and they will emerge in the spring for a full season of growth before the leaves are harvested for the winter. Favorites include: Parsley, Sage, Rosemary, Thyme, Chives, Tarragon, Lovage, Oregano, and Mint.

⑪ Peas

When it comes to growing peas, it's a tough decision whether to grow the classic English podded shell with two rows of tender peas inside, or the flat snow pea used for stir-fry and dips. Before sowing seed, be sure to set up a pea trellis, then roll the seeds in inoculants that will trigger the nitrogen in their DNA and will increase your luscious yields. (These are available through garden centers or seed catalogs.) Sow two seeds about 1 inch deep, planting every 3 to 4 inches along the trellis. Water, and seedlings should emerge within seven days. Flowers will appear, and pods will follow. Favorites: Waverex, Lincoln, Sugar Snap, Carouby de Maussane.

13 Tomatoes

Build ornamental teepees with bamboo poles, or invest in rugged tomato cages to keep tomato plants upright. Focus on heirloom varieties that offer you a range of colors and flavors that go beyond the ordinary. The real secret to a delectable tomato is selecting a variety that suits your climate. Prestart seeds in individual small pots four to six weeks before the frost-free date and transplant when temperatures are steadily above freezing. Mulch the base of the plants with straw to prevent water from splashing soil onto the bottom leaves, which can cause soil-borne disease. Keep suckers trimmed to just the branches that have fruit. Favorites: Sun Gold Cherry, Red or Green Zebra, Persimmon, Big Rainbow, Garden Peach, Brandywine.

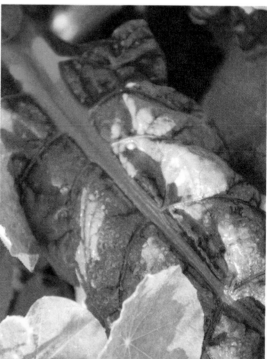

Red Tomato Gazpacho

A blender makes a smooth gazpacho with a quick push of the button, but the hand-chopped version has a chunkier texture that I find more satisfying. You are bound to notice the difference when you make this traditional summer soup with your own homegrown veggies. Garnish with pesto croutons and the most beautiful edible flowers you can find.   *Serves 8*

4 large tomatoes, seeded and finely chopped

1 large cucumber, peeled and finely chopped

1 sweet red onion, finely chopped

1 medium red bell pepper, seeded and finely chopped

1 cup chopped arugula

½ cup chopped fresh sweet basil

½ cup chopped fresh Italian flat-leaf parsley

2 cloves garlic, minced

⅓ cup rice wine or red vinegar

3 tablespoons olive oil

Salt and freshly ground pepper, to taste

Pesto Croutons (see page 229), for garnish

Calendula petals, or other edible flowers, for garnish

1 To make the gazpacho, mix all of the ingredients in a large bowl, or purée them in a blender in batches. Add ice cubes or additional liquid, if desired. Cover and refrigerate until well chilled, at least 4 hours and preferably overnight.

2 Serve the soup in chilled bowls, seasoned with salt and pepper. Garnish with pesto croutons (see page 229), and scatter with calendula petals.

Rainbow Tomatoes with Lemon Basil Dressing

This simple dish is a wonderful way to show off multicolored heirloom tomatoes from your garden. It's especially nice to overlap slices of red, yellow, green zebra, and purple tomatoes, scattered with the finest shreds of lemon basil for a hint of citrus. Add layers of mozzarella and serve with crusty bruschetta for an appetizer. *Serves 4*

6 large ripe tomatoes, preferably three different colors

8 large fresh sweet basil leaves

8 lemon basil leaves

½ pound freshly made mozzarella cheese

¼ cup extra virgin olive oil

Juice of 1 lemon

Coarse sea salt, to taste

Freshly ground pepper, to taste

1 Cut the tomatoes into ½-inch-thick rounds. In a shallow dish with a 1-inch rim, arrange the rounds, slightly overlapping, in a single layer.

2 Chiffonade the basil and scatter over the top. Thinly slice the mozzarella and insert pieces in between the tomatoes.

3 Whisk together the olive oil and the lemon juice, and season with salt and pepper. Pour the dressing evenly over the tomatoes, cover loosely, and let stand at room temperature to marinate for up to 30 minutes. Serve with warm bruschetta.

Creamed Kohlrabi

To many cooks, kohlrabi is an odd vegetable. The green knobs look like turnips, but have a sweet flavor distinctly their own. Young, tender kohlrabi can be sliced or shredded and served raw in salads; larger ones are delicious creamed. This dish is intended to serve four people, but it is so delicious it just might end up serving only two. *Serves 4*

2 large green or purple kohlrabi

1 teaspoon sea salt, plus more to taste

4 tablespoons (½ stick) unsalted butter

3 tablespoons heavy cream

1 teaspoon finely chopped fresh thyme

Freshly ground pepper, to taste

Sprigs of summery savory or marjoram, for garnish

1 Strip the top and root ends from the kohlrabi. Using a paring knife, remove the skin. Grate the kohlrabi on the large holes of a box grater or in a food processor fitted with a grating disk. You should have about 4 cups. Toss the kohlrabi in a colander with the salt. Let stand in a sink to drain off juices, about 30 minutes. Rinse well under cold water. A handful at a time, squeeze out the excess liquid.

2 In a medium skillet, melt the butter over medium heat. Add the kohlrabi and the onion and cover. Cook, stirring occasionally, until the onion is softened, about 5 minutes. Uncover and cook, stirring occasionally, until the kohlrabi is golden brown, about 5 minutes. Stir in the cream and thyme, and cook until the cream is absorbed, about 1 minute. Season with pepper. Serve hot, garnished with sprigs of fresh summer herbs.

Ginger Peach Chutney

Sweet with the summer flavor of ripe peaches and an undertone of warm spiciness that only ginger can provide, this chutney will turn simple grilled chicken into a work of art. Give a few jars away for gifts, but be sure to keep plenty for your own pantry. *Makes 8 pint jars*

2 cups dark brown sugar

2 cups apple cider vinegar

1 fresh cayenne pepper

1 fresh jalapeño

1 tablespoon salt

1 tablespoon mustard seed

1 onion, thinly sliced

4 pounds fresh just-ripe peaches (about 16)

½ cup dried cranberries or raisins

¼ cup fresh grated ginger (3-inch knob) or finely chopped crystallized ginger

1 In a large kettle, combine the sugar and the vinegar and bring to a simmer over medium heat, until the sugar dissolves. Finely dice the cayenne and jalapeño, removing and discarding the seeds. (Take care not to touch your eyes or face while doing so; wash your hands and the knife carefully when done.) Add the salt, mustard seed, and onion. Simmer for about 15 minutes, while you prepare the peaches.

2 Bring a kettle of water to a boil and drop in the peaches. Remove after one minute, cool slightly, and slip off the skins. Cut into slices and then roughly chop into ½- to 1-inch pieces. (There will be about 10 cups of chopped peaches, although an exact amount is not necessary.) Drain the excess juice that will collect in the bottom of the bowl (it is a wonderful sweet nectar for the cook to drink!) and add the peaches to the simmering vinegar brine. Stir in the cranberries or raisins and the ginger.

3 Bring the mixture to a simmer over medium-low heat and allow to cook for about 45 minutes, stirring occasionally, until the peaches and the brine take on a glossy look. Take care not to overcook the peaches, because they will cook again once the canning jars are processed, and it is best to have chunks remain.

4 Once you've deemed the chutney is ready, follow the guidelines on pages 240–241 and safely can the bounty. Label the jars and set them on a shelf for a minimum of 3 months to allow the flavors to meld and ripen.

Rainbow Chard Enchiladas

These chard enchiladas are my healthy dinner solution for when there is an abundance of leafy greens in the garden. Whether you choose to use chard, spinach, or kale, these enchiladas are both sweet and spicy. *Serves 6*

10 cups packed fresh chard, spinach, or kale, washed

2 tablespoons olive oil, plus extra for baking dish and skillet

2 medium onions, coarsely chopped

1 clove garlic, finely chopped

1 medium red or green bell pepper, seeds removed and coarsely chopped

1 jalapeño or other hot pepper, finely chopped (with or without seeds)

6 corn or wheat tortillas

2 cups grated sharp cheddar cheese

2 cups Tomato Maple Salsa (see page 232)

1 Bring a large pot of lightly salted water to a boil and add the chard, spinach, or kale. Cook just until softened, about 2 minutes. Drain and rinse under cold water. Gently squeeze out excess moisture and coarsely chop.

2 Heat the oil in a large skillet, preferably nonstick, over medium heat. Add the onions and garlic; cook, stirring occasionally, until golden, about 5 minutes. Add the peppers and cook another 3 minutes, until softened. Stir in the greens and cook over medium heat, stirring to prevent sticking, until the moisture is reduced, about 5 minutes.

3 Preheat the oven to 375°F. Lightly oil a 9-by-13-inch baking dish. Brush a medium skillet with oil and heat over medium heat. One at a time, heat the tortillas, turning once, until they are soft and pliable, about 30 seconds. Repeat this, stacking the tortillas.

4 When ready to fill, spoon about ¼ cup of the chard filling in the center of a tortilla, and top with about 2 tablespoons cheese. Roll up and place seam side down in the baking dish. Repeat with the remaining tortillas, filling, and cheese.

5 Spread the salsa over the top and sprinkle with the remaining cheese. Bake until the salsa is bubbling and the cheese is melted, about 25 minutes. Serve warm.

Sugar Snap Peas with Poached Scrod en Papillote

Wrap your food in parchment paper, and you are entitled to use the fancy French term *en papillote*, which means "in an envelope." This method allows the ingredients to cook in their own juices, exchanging flavors in the process. In this light but utterly delicious recipe, scrod is melded with sugar snap peas and baby carrots. Serve with brown rice seasoned with herb butter. *Serves 6*

1½ pounds scrod,
    cut into 6 even pieces

1 teaspoon coarse sea salt

½ teaspoon freshly ground pepper

2 tablespoons unsalted butter, chilled,
    cut into 12 thin slices

2 shallots, finely chopped
    (about 4 tablespoons)

12 sugar snap peas, cut into halves
    on the diagonal

12 baby carrots, julienned

1 red bell pepper, seeded and sliced
    into 12 thin wedges

1 lemon, sliced into 6 thin rounds

12 sprigs fresh thyme

6 tablespoons dry white wine

Edible flowers, for garnish

1 Position a rack in the top third of the oven and preheat to 400°F.

2 Season the fish on both sides with the salt and pepper and set aside.

3 Cut out six 8-by-8-inch squares of parchment paper. Fold each in half, then unfold to make a crease in the center. Place 1 piece of butter in the center of one side of the paper. Place a fillet on top of the butter and unevenly sprinkle each piece of fish with shallots, sugar snap peas, carrots, and red pepper slices. Top each with another slice of butter and a lemon slice; add sprigs of fresh thyme and splash each with 1 tablespoon wine.

4 Fold the paper over to enclose the fish and vegetables, and tightly fold the open sides closed by rolling over the edges to seal. Place each of the envelopes on a large baking sheet or roasting pan. Bake for 10–15 minutes, until the paper is well browned.

5 Remove the pan from the oven. Transfer each envelope to a dinner plate, allowing your guests to cut and open them at the table. Or you may open the envelopes and transfer the fish and vegetables to a dinner plate, pour any juices from the envelopes over the fish, and garnish with a nasturtium flower or petals of orange calendula blossoms.

The Children's Garden
Peter Rabbit–Style

Garden Personality: *This garden is a place to play, dig in the soil, spray water, pick spinach and peas, grow flowers, climb, hide, nap, read, and have tea. It is located within the larger garden, and there is only one rule: no adults allowed.*

Form follows function in a Children's Garden, and often the child's wishes are quite different from the parent's. Most children prefer to have their own garden space, and it's ideal to integrate a space for a Children's Garden into the larger family garden. If your kids are young, they will most likely enjoy a place to dig, spray water, and climb, so why not build a sandbox into the corner or a tree house nearby? If your kids are older, they might need magnets such as blueberries, strawberries, or raspberries to entice them to step inside the garden gate.

The best way for children to learn how to garden is by imitating your actions, and together you can share the daily garden routines and explore the world beyond the plants. Be prepared to answer lots of questions: Why do earthworms eat the soil? What is a good bug? How are honeybees helping the garden? Since young children don't understand activities such as weeding or planting in straight rows, give them tasks that will trigger their curiosity and build their connections to the natural world, rather than jobs with merely practical purposes. Above all, keep it fun, and provide gentle guidance without expectations.

Spoil your children and let them graze before dinner on tender garden spinach or snack on sugar snap peas, but be warned that eating fresh from the garden is guaranteed to turn them into food snobs. Supermarket produce and frozen peas from a bag will never hold the same appeal again. Planning a Children's Garden involves the whole family, and a good place to start is at the dinner table. Discuss what foods can be grown, and how long it might take for a head of broccoli to mature. Kids will appreciate the food on their plates far more when they've spent a whole summer nurturing it from seed. Plan to grow crops that have a "wow" factor, such as giant pumpkins, or carrots that mysteriously grow underground, or Easter egg–colored potatoes.

When kids are young, never allow them to think they are in the garden to "work." Always keep it fun and full of little games, such as a strawberry-picking competition or finding the largest bean or the tallest vine. Let the kids help out with planting and weeding—give up the notion that the garden has to be perfect and neat. In the Children's Garden, there should be plenty of pathways so little feet won't step in the soil, and a fence should protect the area from roving chickens or dogs. And if you have time to start a Children's Garden at your children's school, it will help their teachers integrate a natural way to teach math, English, science, art, and ecology, as well as healthier ways to eat.

Ten Tips for Growing a Children's Garden

1 Talk to your kids about what seeds need to grow—soil, sunlight, water—and how long plants take to mature—salads grow quickly, in 30 to 45 days, while broccoli and cauliflower can take 120 days.

2 Assign different roles for each family member, so that everyone has a job and a way to contribute to the family meal.

3 Teach by example, and show children proper techniques for planting, weeding, and harvesting.

4 Keep the garden organic, and reduce the need to use any chemicals.

5 Encourage children to eat fresh from the garden as often as they like—and keep the garden fun!

6 If you build raised beds, select untreated wood such as natural cedar, cypress, or other long-lasting wood; or find a source for local logs. Avoid plastic, since it can leach into the soil.

7 Select a path material that fits your lifestyle and protects tender bare feet. Small pea stone has a neat appearance, but it is not as soft as grass or hay.

8 Never use any chemical herbicide for removing weeds or turf when you start to build your garden.

9 Help your children learn that meals from the family garden are based on what's in season, unlike the timelessness of the supermarket.

10 Add places to relax and flop in the shade, such as a hammock, teepees made by runner beans, or a treehouse.

OVERALL SIZE: *15 feet by 15 feet*
BED SIZE: *(2) beds divided into thirds*
CENTER BED: *6 feet*
PATH WIDTH: *3 feet*
PATH MATERIAL: *Fieldstone for stepping-stones*
FENCE: *Front and back; split-rail for growing peas*

Children's Garden Plant List

1. Beans: Hyacinth Bean (ornamental)
2. Blueberry bushes
3. Carrots: Parmex / Radishes: d'Avignon
4. Marigolds: Lemon Gem
5. Melons: Moon and Stars
6. Onions: Top-Setting Walking Onion
7. Peas: Sugar Snap
8. Potatoes: Mixed Colors
9. Pumpkins: Cinderella
10. Spinach and lettuce
11. Strawberries: Mixed Everlasting
12. Sunflowers: Teddy Bear
13. Tomatoes: Sun Gold Cherry

4 Edible Marigolds

Tagetes tenuifolia is a single blossom marigold that is quite different than the common marigold. These ferny mounds of lemon-scented foliage provide a long blooming season for the kitchen gardener. They are ideal as an edging plant, though they will grow to 12 inches high. Start seeds indoors and transplant into the kitchen garden after danger of frost is past. Seeds can be direct sown, in a single row or broadcast in a block; allow 6 to 8 inches between rows in order to cultivate. Keep plants watered and harvest sprigs of flowers frequently to encourage growth. Favorites: Lemon Gem, Tangerine, Deep Red.

5 Melons

Reserving a small corner of the garden for melons is worthwhile, especially if you live in a temperate climate. Start seeds in small individual pots 4 to 6 weeks before the frost-free date and transplant into hills of three plants each when temperatures are solidly above freezing. Keep plants watered, and trim off branches that do not contain flowers, to concentrate the plant's energy on ripening the fruit. Favorites: Charentais, Galia, Ogen, Blenheim Orange, Moon and Stars.

7 Peas

I've become a fan of the edible pod, especially Sugar Snaps. Before sowing seeds, be sure to set up a pea trellis, then roll the seeds in inoculants that will trigger the nitrogen in

their DNA and increase yields. (Inoculants are available through garden centers or seed catalogs.) Sow two seeds about 1 inch deep, planting every 3 to 4 inches along the trellis. Favorites: Waverex, Lincoln, Sugar Snap, Carouby de Maussane.

⑧ Potatoes

It's hard to resist growing potatoes in a kitchen garden; however, they take up so much room that unless you have extra growing space, it's best to limit your choices to those specialty potatoes that are otherwise hard to find. Order seed potatoes from a reliable source, cut each potato into sections that include an eye, and plant underground. Favorites: Yukon Gold, German Fingerling, Butte, Carola, Rose Gold, Russian Banana, Caribe.

⑫ Sunflowers

Helianthus annuus is not a single flower, but a grouping of numerous florets inside a circular disc. The outer petals can be yellow, maroon, or orange and eventually mature into seeds that feed the birds. Sunflowers most commonly grow to between 5 and 12 feet tall, depending on the variety. Easily grown by seed indoors or directly in the garden, select a variety of heights and colors for a full range. Favorites: Italian White, Autumn Beauty, Moulin Rouge, Sunbright, Zebulon, Velvet Queen.

Ginger Carrot Soup with Creamy Lime Garnish

Once you've plucked your own carrots from the garden, you'll truly appreciate how different their flavor is from that of their store-bought cousins. This soup has both a rich color and a spicy, fragrant scent. *Serves 6*

2 tablespoons olive oil

2 tablespoons unsalted butter

2 shallots, minced

2 cloves garlic, minced

1 teaspoon salt

¼ cup chopped crystallized ginger

½ teaspoon turmeric

¼ teaspoon cinnamon

1 teaspoon curry powder

1 pinch freshly ground pepper

8 carrots, trimmed and sliced into coins (about 3 cups)

5 cups vegetable broth

1 cup apple cider

1 cup vanilla yogurt

Zest of 1 lime

Fresh herbs, for garnish

1 In a 4-quart stockpot, heat the oil and butter over medium heat. Add the shallots, garlic, and salt. Reduce the heat to low and cook for 5 minutes, stirring, until softened. (Shallots brown more easily than onions, so keep an eye on them. But even if they turn a dark brown, they are still delicious in this soup.)

2 Stir in the ginger and the other spices. Cook for about 5 minutes to allow the fragrant oils from the spices to release. Stir in the carrots, and cook for another 5 minutes for the vegetables to absorb all the flavors.

3 Pour in the vegetable broth and cider to cover with about 1 inch to spare. Cover, lower the heat, and simmer the soup for about 45 minutes, until everything is tender. Test for doneness by spearing the larger pieces with a sharp knife.

4 Remove from heat, and purée with an immersion blender to a smooth consistency. In a small bowl, combine the yogurt with the lime zest. Serve the soup warm with a dollop of yogurt and a garnish of fresh herbs.

Blueberry-Zucchini Bread

In most gardens, the blueberries ripen just as the zucchini is starting to get big, so the two are natural partners for a tasty quick bread. Zucchini bread is a familiar way to celebrate the annual profusion of summer squash. Smother this bread with sweet blueberry syrup as a breakfast treat or a light dessert. *Makes one 9-by-12-inch cake or one loaf*

3 cups unbleached all-purpose flour

1 teaspoon ground cinnamon

1 teaspoon baking soda

¼ teaspoon baking powder

1 teaspoon sea salt

1½ cups sugar

12 tablespoons (1½ sticks) unsalted butter, softened

3 large eggs

1 teaspoon pure vanilla extract

½ cup plain yogurt

2 cups grated zucchini (about 3 medium zucchini)

1 tablespoon lemon zest

1 pint fresh blueberries

BLUEBERRY SAUCE

1 pint fresh blueberries

Juice of 1 lemon

1 tablespoon lemon zest

¼ cup sugar

1 cinnamon stick

½ cup water

1 Preheat the oven to 350°F. Position a rack in the center of the oven. Lightly butter and flour a 9-by-12-inch baking pan or bread loaf pan, tapping out the excess flour.

2 In a large bowl, combine the flour, cinnamon, baking soda, baking powder, and salt. Set aside.

3 In the large bowl of an electric mixer, beat the sugar and butter on high speed until smooth.

4 Add the eggs, one at a time, beating well after each addition. Reduce the speed to low and beat in the vanilla and yogurt. Gradually add the flour mixture until combined.

5 With a wooden spoon, fold in the zucchini, lemon zest, and blueberries and stir gently until the ingredients are just blended. Pour into the floured pan and tap on the counter to even the batter.

6 Bake until a toothpick inserted in the center of the loaf comes out clean, 45 minutes to 1 hour. Cool in the pan on a wire rack for 10 minutes.

7 While the cake is cooking, combine all the sauce ingredients in a small saucepan and slowly bring to a boil. Reduce the heat and simmer until the blueberries soften. Spoon over the warm bread.

Tricolor Scalloped Potatoes

The blue potato, a direct descendant of the original potato from the Andes Mountains, is rugged and hardy, and kids love them mashed. In truth, their flavor isn't as good as that of other varieties. To remedy this drawback, I often match them up with their cousins, as in this updated version of the classic dish with blue, white, and yellow potatoes. Cut the potatoes into rounds of an even thickness, use a food processor fitted with a grate, or a hand grater or mandoline.   *Serves 6*

6 tablespoons (¾ stick) unsalted butter, melted

3 cloves garlic, minced

4 medium new potatoes, scrubbed and sliced into ⅛-inch-thick rounds

4 small blue potatoes, scrubbed and sliced into ⅛-inch-thick rounds

4 small Yukon gold potatoes, scrubbed and sliced into ⅛-inch-thick rounds

1 teaspoon chopped fresh thyme or rosemary

1 teaspoon sea salt

½ teaspoon freshly ground pepper

1 cup heavy cream, heated to just under boiling

1 cup shredded Gruyère cheese

Fresh Italian flat-leaf parsley or thyme, for garnish

1 Position a rack in the center of the oven and preheat to 425°F. Lightly butter a 9-by-13-inch deep baking pan or casserole.

2 Mix the melted butter with the garlic. Arrange a layer of potatoes, alternating colors, in the baking pan. Drizzle with half the garlic butter and season with half the thyme or rosemary, and half the salt and pepper. Repeat with the remaining potatoes, garlic butter, thyme, salt, and pepper. Pour the cream over the potatoes and sprinkle with the cheese. Cover with foil and bake for 30 minutes.

3 Uncover the pan and continue to bake until the potatoes are tender when pierced with a fork and the top is a deep golden brown, another 15 minutes. Let stand for a few minutes, then serve hot. Garnish with the parsley or thyme.

Fresh Fennel Salsa over Herb-Crusted Haddock

Fennel is one of the best friends a fish can have in the kitchen. When you combine this haddock with a salsa of tomatillos, fennel, and aromatic Thai basil, the result is a dinner that could only come from your own kitchen garden. Serve this simple herbed fish with steamed brown rice, colorful broccoli florets, and a dry white wine. *Serves 4*

1½ cups fresh bread crumbs

1 teaspoon fresh thyme, finely chopped

1 teaspoon fresh tarragon, finely chopped

1 teaspoon fresh savory, finely chopped

1½ pounds haddock fillets, cut into 4 pieces

Salt and freshly ground black pepper, to taste

4 tablespoons olive oil

2 tablespoons unsalted butter

3 tablespoons freshly grated Parmesan cheese

Fresh Fennel and Tomatillo Salsa (see below)

1 Preheat the oven to 350°F.

2 In a bowl, combine the bread crumbs with the thyme, tarragon, and savory. Season the fish with salt and pepper and coat with the bread-crumb mixture.

3 Heat the oil and butter in a large nonstick skillet over medium-high heat. Add the fish and cook on both sides until golden, about 3 minutes. Transfer to a baking pan and sprinkle with the Parmesan cheese. Bake for 10 minutes.

4 Serve on warm plates with fennel salsa.

Fresh Fennel and Tomatillo Salsa

1 tablespoon olive oil

1 Walla Walla sweet onion, finely chopped

1 small fennel bulb, trimmed and chopped

1 cup golden tomatillos (cape gooseberries)

2 ripe tomatoes, halved, seeded, and chopped

2 cloves garlic, finely chopped

¼ cup kalamata olives, pitted and chopped

1 teaspoon finely chopped fresh Thai basil

1 teaspoon finely chopped fresh Italian flat-leaf parsley

Salt and freshly ground pepper, to taste

In a large nonstick skillet, heat the olive oil over medium-high heat. Sauté the onion and fennel until soft, about 5 minutes. Add the tomatillos, tomatoes, garlic, olives, basil, and parsley. Season with salt and pepper. Cook for another 5 minutes, stirring frequently.

Pumpkin Tart with Amaretto Cream-Cheese Crust

This is a nice twist on traditional pumpkin pie; the blend of almond and coconut milk with a splash of rum gives this richly flavored pumpkin tart a tropical burst. Serve a small wedge with a cup of chai as an afternoon treat, or after dinner for a petite dessert. *Makes two 9-inch tarts*

CRUST

4 tablespoons unsalted butter

4 tablespoons cream cheese

2 tablespoons vegetable shortening

1 cup white all-purpose flour

1 teaspoon almond extract

1 teaspoon sugar

½ teaspoon salt

3 tablespoons ice water, or less as needed

TOPPING

12 Italian amaretto ladyfingers

¼ cup toasted slivered almonds

1 tablespoon amaretto or 2 teaspoons almond extract

FILLING

1½ cups cooked and puréed pumpkin

½ cup granulated sugar

½ cup dark brown sugar

3 tablespoons dark rum

1 tablespoon unsulphured molasses

1 teaspoon ground cinnamon

¼ teaspoon ground ginger

¼ teaspoon ground cloves

3 large eggs

1 cup lite coconut milk

1 Prepare the crust: Cut the butter, cream cheese, and vegetable shortening into ½-inch cubes and place in the freezer 1 hour prior to making the dough. In a food processor, blend the flour, sugar, and salt to combine. Add the butter, cream cheese, and short-ening, piece by piece, pulsing to break up the chunks into pea-size pieces. Transfer the mixture to a medium bowl and add the almond extract and just enough ice water to create a cohesive ball. Cut into 2 balls, wrap each in wax paper, and press each into a 5-inch disk. Refrigerate for 1 hour.

2 Prepare the topping: Combine the topping ingredients in a food processor fitted with a steel blade. Pulse until crumbled into cornmeal-size pieces. Transfer to a bowl and set aside.

3 Prepare the filling: In the bowl of an electric mixer, combine the pumpkin, granulated sugar, brown sugar, rum, molasses, cin-namon, ginger, and cloves and blend until the brown sugar dissolves. Beat in the eggs, one at a time, then add the coconut milk and blend.

4 Preheat the oven to 350°F. Remove the dough from the refrigerator; let stand for 5 minutes to soften slightly. On a lightly floured surface, roll one disk into a 10-inch round, about ¼ inch thick. Fold the dough in half, place in a 9-inch tart pan, and gently press the dough into the sides. Trim the excess crust by rolling the top edge with the back of a spoon or the rolling pin, so that the top of the crust meets the top of the tart pan. Repeat the process for the second tart.

5 Place the tart pans on a baking sheet and pour the filling evenly into the crusts. Sprinkle on the topping and bake for 40 minutes. The custard center may still appear to be moist, but it will become more solid as the pie cools. Transfer to a wire rack and cool. Remove the outside rims of the tart pans, and serve at room temperature or chilled.

The Culinary Herb Garden
Fresh and Flavorful

Garden Personality: *The relatively carefree nature of herbs, along with their aromatic qualities, makes this garden ideal for an entrance or pathway into the house. Fill your Culinary Herb Garden with color, texture, and fragrance; a showy blend of green, gray, and gold will rival a flower border for visual beauty and surpass it in usefulness.*

The herb family comprises hundreds of species, and learning which ones are the best for your own kitchen garden may take a few seasons. Herb cultivars fall into two main categories: annuals and perennials. Annual herb plants live a single season, with a focused goal to set seed. Perennials go dormant when the temperatures drop, and generate new foliage during the growing season. Ideally your herb garden will contain a mixture of both, in order to make it easier to get to know the different plants.

As you learn to cook with herbs, you may wish to keep expanding your herb garden plant list, especially when you discover pineapple sage, lemon basil, or chocolate mint. If you love basil, you can choose from more than eighty different cultivars and fill a single garden with sweet, scented, or sacred basil. Love the smell of lemon thyme? Check out the dozens of varieties, from low-creeping thyme to variegated thyme, both ideal for forming garden edges or enhancing paths. The most successful herb gardens may appear carefree, yet they require the most planning in order to get the design right from the start.

The term "herb" encompasses a wide spectrum of delicate soft-stemmed annuals, woody perennials, and large voracious plants that also double as gorgeous ornamentals. Many herbs remain compact, but others are prone to spread underground with an active root system that can easily turn into a weed. Do your research and get to know your herbs before you welcome them into your herb garden.

Ten Tips for Growing a Culinary Herb Garden

1 It's important to learn which plants will become weedy, and keep them from spreading. Avoid planting mint in the herb garden; grow it separately in a pot.

2 Most herbs thrive in terrain that resembles the Mediterranean, with dry, sandy soil and full, beating sun. Good drainage is essential for their roots; if you have standing water in your garden area, be prepared to dig ditches.

3 Before you plant, be certain the soil is completely weed free, or you will lose the battle quickly. Since herbs grow rapidly, they will harbor weeds in their root systems that are often hard to find until the fall.

4 Go light on feeding herbs with fertilizer or nutrient-rich compost, since an overdose of nitrogen will diminish the essential oils in their leaves.

5 Most perennial herb seeds take a long time to germinate. Plan to purchase established plants whenever possible.

6 Annual herbs are easier to start from seed. For best results, direct sow dill, basil, and cilantro.

7 Cook with your fresh herbs as often as possible, and learn the classic combinations that work well together in cuisine. Plan to replace your dried herbs each winter to keep their flavors vibrant.

8 Honeybees love an herb garden, and will also pollinate your vegetable garden and fruit trees, as well as your neighbor's gardens. Consider becoming a beekeeper.

9 Unless you are growing your herbs exclusively as ornamentals, harvest herbs before a flower appears in order to capture the most potent essential oils in the leaves.

10 At the end of the season, harvest your herbs. For perennials, clip a few inches above the ground, leaving enough of the stem to regenerate new growth during the remaining part of the growing season. For annuals, harvest just before a killing frost, and remove the roots from the garden.

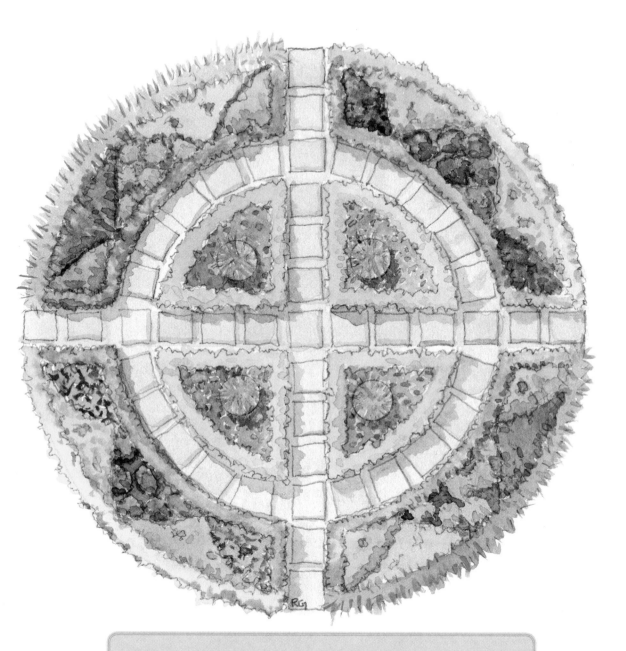

OVERALL SIZE: *18 feet by 18 feet (circular)*
BED SIZE: *3 feet outer circle / 2 feet inner circle*
PATH WIDTH: *2 feet central path / 3 feet main path*
RAISED BED: *Granite stone blocks*
PATH MATERIAL: *Bluestone squares with crushed gravel*

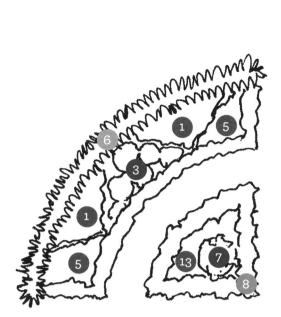
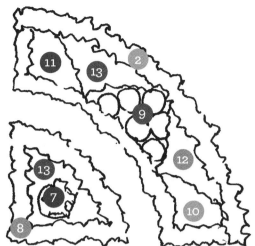
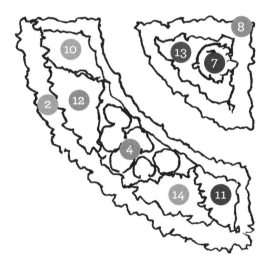

Culinary Herb Garden Plant List

1. Basil: Sweet Genovese and Mammoth
2. Bee Balm: Panorama Red
3. Borage
4. Chives: Garlic
5. Cilantro: Santo
6. Dill: Fernleaf
7. Lavender: Munstead (cool climate) or Lady (warm climate)

8. Parsley: Italian Flat-Leaf
9. Rosemary: Upright
10. Sage: Bergarten
11. Summer Savory
12. Tarragon: French
13. Thyme: Lemon
14. Marjoram

Basil

The basil family comprises close to eighty different types, although only about a dozen are used for culinary purposes. A tender annual, basil is easily started from seed or purchased as a plant; it thrives on heat and full sun. Start with a classic sweet basil, then add scented basil, reserving the miniature basil for a border plant. Start seeds indoors and transplant into prepared loose soil outdoors after the danger of frost is past. Or direct sow seeds into prepared soil, either in a single row or broadcast in a block; allow 6 to 8 inches between rows in order to cultivate. Favorites: Sweet Genovese, Fine Green, Red Rubin, Mammoth, Lemon, Cinnamon, Dark Opal, Thai.

⑤ Cilantro

Direct sow seeds for high productivity. Keep seed heads harvested to allow a longer season for the foliage, or allow seeds to develop, which will produce coriander. Spicy and fragrant, cilantro leaves are a unique flavoring that make an excellent fresh salsa or guacamole.

⑥ Dill

As with cilantro, direct sow seeds for best results and a long season of delicate, ferny foliage to complement salads, fish, and cheese. Keep seed heads harvested to cultivate longer-lasting plants.

(9) Rosemary

Rosemary is a woody herb with fragrant evergreen needlelike leaves. It prefers soil with good drainage in an open, sunny area. Rosemary is easily pruned into shapes and grown in pots. It can be propagated from seed but takes a long time to germinate, so it is best to purchase plants from a nursery. Select the classic upright form for the best culinary properties.

(10) Sage

Sage is a member of the large Artemisia family, and is prized in the culinary herb garden for its soft, blue-green foliage as much as for its pungent flavor. Particularly useful in chicken and egg dishes, sage can be grown easily in most conditions. Since sage takes a long time to germinate from seed, select plants from a local nursery. Harvest leaves throughout the summer to encourage bushy growth, and in the fall to hang dry for soups and stews.

(12) Tarragon

French tarragon is cultivated by root division rather than by seed so it is best to purchase a plant and place it in a hot, sunny spot, without excessive watering. Tarragon prefers poor soil and produces aromatic leaves from early spring onward. Tarragon is one of the four *fines herbes* of French cooking, and is particularly suitable for chicken and fish. It may also be steeped in vinegar for use on salads.

Parmesan Herb Popovers

Popovers are the ultimate breakfast treat, eggy and warm. I like to serve them for dinner, too, and I make this variation to serve alongside butternut squash soup or a winter stew. Preheating the popover pan ensures the pastries rise and "pop over" the sides. *Makes 6 popovers*

3 tablespoons unsalted butter

¾ cup flour

½ teaspoon salt

¼ teaspoon freshly ground pepper

1 teaspoon finely chopped fresh rosemary

2 tablespoons finely chopped fresh parsley

3 eggs

1 cup whole milk

½ cup freshly grated Parmesan cheese

1 Preheat the oven to 400°F. Dot each of six popover cups with ½ tablespoon butter and place in the hot oven to preheat while you mix the batter.

2 In a small bowl, blend together the flour, salt, pepper, rosemary, and parsley. Set aside.

3 In a mixing bowl, beat together the eggs, add the milk and cheese, then fold in the flour mixture and beat until smooth.

4 Once the popover cups are heated and the butter is thoroughly melted, remove the cups from the oven and divide the batter evenly into each cup.

5 Return to the oven and bake for 25 minutes, until the popovers are golden brown. Remove from the oven and serve warm.

Basil Pesto

Pesto has many uses that go beyond pasta. Spoon it over steamed vegetables, turn it into a marinade for chicken or fish, or use this basic recipe for your own variations, adding a bit of scented basil, oregano, rosemary, or other herbs as you wish. *Makes 1½ cups*

2 cloves garlic, coarsely chopped

2 cups packed fresh basil leaves, rinsed and towel-dried

1 cup packed fresh Italian flat-leaf parsley

¼ cup pine nuts, toasted

¼ cup freshly grated Parmigiano-Reggiano cheese

½ cup extra virgin olive oil

Salt and freshly ground pepper, to taste

In the bowl of a food processor, combine the garlic, basil, parsley, and pine nuts. Purée until blended. Add the cheese and pulse to combine. With the motor running, slowly add the oil to make a creamy paste. Season with salt and pepper.

Basil-Wrapped Grilled Fish

Mammoth basil leaves grow as large as your hand and are well suited for wrapping fish fillets or other quick-cooking foods for the grill. The leaves impart a delicate flavor to the fish and help keep the flesh moist while cooking. Soak the leaves in cold water to keep the basil from scorching on the grill. Experiment by substituting other scented basil leaves, such as lemon or cinnamon, for variations in flavor. *Serves 4*

8 mammoth basil leaves

1½ pounds skinless scrod fillets

¼ teaspoon salt

½ teaspoon freshly ground pepper

4 tablespoons Basil Pesto (see page 102)

1 lemon, cut into 8 thin slices

8 wooden skewers or toothpicks, soaked in water for 30 minutes

1 Light a charcoal fire in an outdoor grill and let it burn until the coals are covered with white ash. (Or preheat a gas grill on low heat.) While the fire is heating, soak the basil leaves in a bowl of cold water.

2 Cut the fillets vertically into 8 strips, each about 2 inches wide. Season the strips with the salt and pepper. Spread the pesto on the strips and top each with a lemon slice. Drain the basil leaves, shaking off most of the water. Wrap each strip in a wet basil leaf and secure with a toothpick or skewer.

3 Lightly oil the grill, place the fish on the grill, and cover. Cook until the fish is completely cooked in the center when cut with a sharp knife, about 10 minutes. Remove the leaves, and serve hot.

Cook's Note

Basil loses its zip when it is refrigerated or frozen. If you freeze pesto for the winter, try blanching the basil before freezing to keep the green color and fresh flavor: Measure 2 cups basil leaves and drop them into boiling salted water. Cook just until wilted, less than a minute. Drain in a colander and pat dry. Make pesto on page 102, and freeze in small containers. Before using, defrost at room temperature.

Tarragon Chicken Salad with Creamy Blue Cheese Dressing

A main-dish salad layered with flavors, this delivers the best of the herb garden along with the wonderfully warm, creamy flavors of blue cheese, honey, and tarragon. *Serves 4*

1 clove garlic, minced

2 tablespoons olive oil

1 cup whole-milk Greek-style yogurt

2 tablespoons finely chopped fresh tarragon, or 1 tablespoon dried

3 boneless skinless chicken breasts (about 1½ pounds)

Salt and pepper, to taste

½ cup walnuts

1 head soft butterhead lettuce, torn into bite-size pieces

½ head radicchio, thinly sliced or cut into chiffonade

1 cup arugula or mixed greens, washed and chilled

Creamy Blue Cheese Dressing (see facing page)

1 Preheat the oven to 350°F.

2 In a glass bowl, toss together the garlic, olive oil, yogurt, and tarragon. Season the chicken breasts lightly with salt and pepper, place in the bowl with the yogurt mixture, and toss to coat. Arrange the chicken in a single layer in an open baking dish; spoon the yogurt mixture over the chicken, covering every surface. Bake for 35 minutes, basting midway to keep the chicken moist.

3 Place the walnuts in another open dish alongside the chicken, and bake for 10 minutes. Remove both dishes from the oven and cool.

4 In a large salad bowl, toss the lettuce, radicchio, and arugula or mixed greens with the creamy blue cheese dressing, to taste. Neatly arrange on four separate salad plates, topping evenly with thinly sliced baked chicken. Finely chop the walnuts, dividing between each salad, and serve.

Herb Cheese Spread

The best time to make this savory cheese spread is, of course, in the summer, when fresh herbs are abundant. This is a family favorite and we find many uses for it. Served with a mound of crisp, fresh vegetables and crackers, it is a light and tasty lunch. At other times, it serves as a filling for cherry tomatoes or snow peas, or even as a spread on a roast beef sandwich. Try to make it a day before to allow the flavors to meld. Garnish the spread with nasturtium flowers—not only are they pretty, but they also add a dash of mild spiciness to the cheese.   *Makes 1 cup*

2 cloves garlic, peeled

2 tablespoons chopped fresh basil

2 tablespoons chopped fresh dill

1 tablespoon chopped fresh chives

One 8-ounce package cream cheese

Nasturtium flowers, for garnish

1 With the back of a knife, smash the garlic to release the oils. Place the garlic in a food processor fitted with a steel blade. Add the herbs and pulse until finely chopped, about 30 seconds.

2 Drop in the cream cheese and pulse until well blended, scraping down the sides of the bowl as needed.

3 Transfer to a small bowl and refrigerate for at least 2 hours. Serve with simple crackers or thinly sliced grilled French bread. Garnish with nasturtium flowers.

Creamy Blue Cheese Dressing   *Makes ½ cup*

2 ounces blue cheese

2 tablespoons red wine vinegar

1 tablespoon finely chopped fresh tarragon, or 1 teaspoon dried

1 tablespoon honey

4–6 tablespoons olive oil

1–2 tablespoons kefir yogurt drink (optional)

Salt and pepper, to taste

With a fork, mash together the blue cheese, vinegar, tarragon, and honey. Drizzle in the olive oil until a smooth paste is formed. For a creamier dressing, add kefir, to taste. Season with salt and pepper.

Summer-Herb Cheese Bread

Making herbed bread is such a simple way to bring the scent of the garden into your kitchen. Baking bread is a forgotten pleasure, and this easy bread recipe is a good place to relearn the basics. The result is golden-yellow bread, infused with green herby flecks, that is heavenly sliced for a grilled-cheese sandwich or topped with a thin spread of Boursin cheese or herbed butter. You can substitute cottage cheese for the cheddar, which will yield a soft, moist interior. Try serving this with the Herb Cheese Spread (see page 105). *Makes 1 large loaf*

¼-ounce package (2¼ teaspoons)
   active dry yeast

1 teaspoon sugar

1½ cups warm (105°F–115°F) water

4 cups unbleached all-purpose flour,
   as needed

1 cup shredded sharp Vermont cheddar
   cheese or cottage cheese

¼ cup finely chopped fresh mixed herbs
   (parsley, sage, rosemary, thyme)

3 tablespoons extra virgin olive oil,
   plus extra for the loaf pan

2 teaspoons salt

½ teaspoon freshly ground pepper

1 Sprinkle the yeast and sugar over the water in a large bowl. Let stand until the mixture looks foamy, about 10 minutes. Stir to dissolve the yeast. Stir in 1 cup of the flour, the cheese, herbs, olive oil, salt, and pepper. Gradually stir in enough flour to make a stiff dough.

2 Turn the dough out onto a lightly floured work surface and knead, adding more flour as required, until the dough is smooth and elastic, about 10 minutes. Gather the dough into a ball. Lightly oil a large bowl. Place the dough in the bowl and turn to coat with the oil. Cover the bowl with a damp kitchen towel, and let stand in a warm place until the dough has doubled in volume, about 1½ hours.

3 Punch the dough, and turn out onto a lightly floured work surface. Lightly oil a large bread loaf pan, and shape the dough to fit inside. Turn the dough over to coat both sides with oil, and cover again with the damp kitchen towel. Let stand in a warm place until doubled in volume, about 45 minutes.

4 Meanwhile, position a rack in the center of the oven and preheat to 375°F. Bake for 45 minutes, or until the loaf sounds hollow on the bottom when tapped. Transfer to a wire rack and cool.

Lemon Ricotta Fritters with Lavender Honey

The batter can be made before dinner, and then it is just a matter of deep-frying the fritters. The reward will be crisp, freshly cooked, melt-in-your-mouth morsels with soft lemony centers, just the thing to dip into fragrant lavender honey. In Provence, the bees that frequent the wild purple-budded bushes growing near their hives make lavender honey. Be aware that this homemade version, infused with lavender flowers, needs to stand for 24 hours before being used. Only your own lavender will do, freshly harvested from the garden. *Serves 4*

LAVENDER HONEY

1 cup raw honey

24 fresh lavender sprigs, with buds

RICOTTA FRITTERS

1 pound whole-milk ricotta cheese

4 large eggs

⅔ cup all-purpose flour

3 tablespoons unsalted butter, melted

2 tablespoons finely chopped fresh lemon verbena or mint

Grated zest of 2 lemons

½ teaspoon sea salt

Vegetable oil for deep-frying

Fresh lemon verbena or mint leaves, for garnish

1 To make the lavender honey, warm the honey in a small saucepan over medium heat. Stir in the lavender. Remove from the heat, cover, and let stand at room temperature for 24 hours. Strain through a sieve into a clean jar.

2 To make the fritters, whisk together the ricotta and eggs, until blended but not quite smooth. Gradually stir in the flour, then fold in the butter, lemon verbena or mint (if using), lemon zest, and salt. Cover the batter with plastic wrap and let stand at room temperature for 1 hour.

3 Position a rack in the center of the oven and preheat to 200°F. Line a baking sheet with paper towels and set aside.

4 Pour enough oil into a large saucepan to come halfway up the sides of the pan. Heat on high until a deep-frying thermometer reads 365°F.

5 In batches, without crowding, drop table-spoons of the batter into the hot oil. Cook, turning once, until the fritters are golden brown, about 3 minutes. Using a wire skimmer or slotted spoon, transfer the fritters to the paper towels and keep warm in the oven while making the remaining fritters.

6 Place a few fritters on each of four plates, drizzle with a generous tablespoon of the lavender honey, and sprinkle with the lemon verbena or mint leaves. Serve hot.

The Paint Box Garden
Raised Beds

Garden Personality: *In this garden, beds are displayed in a decorative pattern to show off an array of ornamental edibles. Instead of all the vibrant colors competing in one large garden, the Paint Box Garden lets you plant by color to create a patchwork quilt with shades of green, textures from ferny to frilly, and dabs of pink, red, and blue around the edges.*

Instead of digging a garden in the earth, create a series of raised beds by stacking wood together to form an enclosed area. Fill it with topsoil or compost and you have an instant garden. This is especially beneficial if your soil is composed of heavy clay or is otherwise difficult to amend for growing vegetables, herbs, and flowers. Raised beds offer several other advantages: They lift plants higher, which protects them from the early spring frost. They are also a deterrent for rabbits and dogs, as well as a natural barrier against grass and weeds.

There are numerous options for what to use for your raised beds; the best materials will be those that are made with untreated, rot-resistant wood. These include cedar, cypress, and any hardwood indigenous to your area that has not been treated with chemicals. Wood will not last forever, but it sure beats plastic, which can leach into the soil, leaving residuals that may affect the health of your crops. Movable raised beds are optimal for gardeners who are renting, or are unsure where to plant a more permanent garden. If you change your mind, simply knock down the sides and stack the wood.

Just as with a traditional garden, give careful thought to where you might place the raised beds to provide the option for full sun exposure and access to water spigots and hoses, but also to how the beds blend into your yard. In this Paint Box Garden, the raised beds are grouped together in a pattern that takes up minimal space, yet provide ample growing opportunities for a range of colorful vegetables.

Ten Tips for Growing a Paint Box Garden

1 Research options for raised beds to determine the best choice for your landscape.

2 Select a level location; clear the land of weeds and turf where the beds will be installed.

3 Set up an irrigation system, or be sure the beds are located near a hose spigot.

4 Fill the beds with a combination of 65 percent screened topsoil, 20 percent compost, 10 percent well-aged manure, and 5 percent peat.

5 The soil should be partially replaced each season to avoid soil-borne disease. Continue to feed the soil each season, with organic fertilizer and compost.

6 Mulch the paths with gravel or bark mulch to keep garden maintenance low.

7 Select plants that are vibrantly colored and that vary in size, height, and texture.

8 Create a boundary around the garden with a row of boxwood or sunflowers.

9 Follow the four-square organic rotation system to determine where to plant each season.

10 Stack the raised beds double high for easier planting and maintenance and less bending over.

OVERALL SIZE: *24 feet by 24 feet*
BED SIZE: *8 feet by 4 feet by 4 feet*
NUMBER OF BEDS: 4
CENTRAL PATH WIDTH: *3 feet*
CENTRAL BED: *4 feet by 4 feet*
PATH MATERIAL: *Bark mulch, grass, or light gravel*

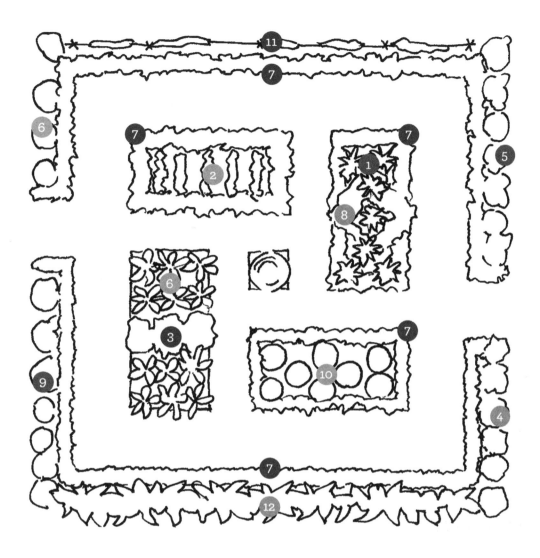

Paint Box Garden Plant List

1 Artichokes: Imperial Star

2 Basil: Red Rubin and Sweet Genovese

3 Beans: Fava

4 Broccoli: Romanesco

5 Brussels Sprouts: Rubine

6 Chard: Rainbow

7 Edible Flowers: Borage, Calendula, Nasturtium, and Amaranth

8 Fennel: Bronze

9 Kale: Black Tuscan

10 Lettuce: Mixed Butterheads

11 Peas: Carouby d'Maussane Snow Pea

12 Sunflowers: The Joker

① Artichokes

In more temperate parts of the country, artichokes are a perennial thistle that originated in southern Europe. They have two major seasons, from February to May and then a shorter one in October. While artichokes can be found in many markets, they are an outstanding ornamental edible. Sow them in pots early and transplant them to the garden.

④ Broccoli

Broccoli can take 80 to 100 days to grow from seed to head, but the kitchen gardener will enjoy flavor and variety that far surpass anything found in the supermarket. Consider growing the remarkable Romanesque broccoli with its twirling spirals of tender shoots or the unusual purple broccoli for a colorful mixed fall salad. Broccoli can be ornamental in the garden, but as soon as the head starts to form, keep an eye on it and be sure to harvest it while it is still green and tight. Favorites: Romanesque, Broccoli Raab, Packman, Green Magic, Gypsy.

⑤ Brussels Sprouts

This is a fall crop that takes close to 125 days to mature, but it is well worth growing for its ornamental quality alone. It is long lasting in the garden; remove the leaves as the sprouts begin to appear on the main stem. Sow seeds in pots in late May, or buy plants and transplant into the garden. Favorites: Oliver, Igor.

8 Fennel

There are several different types of fennel, and it is grown for both its seeds and for the inflated leaf base that forms a bulb. It has a mild anise flavor, and can be eaten raw or cooked. The Italian *Finocchio* is the one to grow for the bulbs, while bronze-leaved fennel is grown as a decorative garden plant. The leaves of both are prized for flavoring fish, soups and salads or as a garnish. Sow seeds indoors in pots, four weeks prior to planting in the garden.

9 Kale

Kale and collards are staples in the garden; they are among the easiest and most satisfying greens to grow and are beautiful plants that provide an abundance of healthy, showy greens. Kale and collards come in a range of varieties, from small, tender-leaved varieties that are ideal for specialty salad mixes, to the more familiar, larger-leaved kale that will stay hardy in lower temperatures and thrive in cool climates late into the fall. They are easy to start from seed, either direct sown in rows allowing 8 inches between plants, or in plug trays to transplant. Cover young plants with floating row covers to prevent flea beetles or pests that can munch holes in the leaves. Harvest outer leaves as needed and keep plants growing late into the fall until severe frost arrives. Favorites: Red Russian, Black Tuscan, Redbor, Winterport.

Rainbow Chard Soup with Rosemary

Rosemary is a favorite in the culinary herb garden, and although its fragrance may seem strong at first, in this soup it offers only a subtle hint that blends nicely with the greens. Keep this soup slightly chunky, with swirls of green and cubes of potato giving it texture. For a smokier flavor, crumble in a garnish of crisp bacon or diced ham. Any greens in season can be substituted for the chard. *Serves 4 to 6*

ROSEMARY CROUTONS

4 slices French-style sourdough bread, cut into ½-inch cubes

⅓ cup extra virgin olive oil

1 clove garlic, minced

1 tablespoon finely chopped fresh or dried rosemary

SOUP

2 tablespoons unsalted butter

2 tablespoons extra virgin olive oil

1 clove garlic, minced

1 medium onion, coarsely chopped (about 1 cup)

1 tablespoon fresh rosemary leaves, finely chopped (or 1 teaspoon dried)

½ teaspoon salt

Freshly ground pepper, to taste

4 red-skinned potatoes, diced (2 cups)

4 cups chicken broth, vegetable stock, or water

6 cups fresh chard or spinach leaves, destalked

Freshly grated nutmeg, to taste

1 Prepare the croutons: Preheat the oven to 375°F. Place the bread cubes in a bowl and toss with the oil, garlic, and rosemary. Spread the cubes in a single layer on a baking sheet and bake for 10 minutes, stirring occasionally, until crisp. Set aside until ready to serve.

2 Prepare the soup: Melt the butter and oil in a heavy-bottomed saucepan over medium heat. Add the garlic, onions, and rosemary, along with the salt and a grinding of pepper. Sweat over a gentle heat for 5 minutes. Stir in the potatoes and cook for 3 minutes. Add the broth and simmer for 15 minutes, until the potatoes are soft. Add the chard or spinach and continue to simmer for 10 minutes. Turn off the heat.

3 With an immersion blender, purée the broth to break up the larger pieces to desired consistency. Serve in warmed bowls, garnished with grated nutmeg and the croutons.

Baked Salmon in Phyllo
with Tomato-Ginger Filling

The next time company comes for dinner, consider these phyllo-wrapped salmon fillets, with a spicy fresh tomato-and-ginger filling. Serve with your favorite hollandaise or aioli. *Serves 4*

4 plum tomatoes, halved, seeded, and cut into fine dice

2 tablespoons peeled and grated fresh ginger

Zest and juice of 1 lime

2 tablespoons finely chopped fresh fennel fronds

¼ teaspoon salt

⅛ teaspoon freshly ground pepper

Oil for baking sheet

8 sheets defrosted phyllo pastry dough

8 tablespoons (1 stick) unsalted butter, melted

1½ pounds salmon, cut into 8 pieces about 2 inches wide

1 In a small bowl, combine the tomatoes, ginger, lime zest and juice, and fennel. Season with the salt and pepper.

2 Lightly oil a baking sheet. Spread out the phyllo dough, and set up a workstation. Using a pastry brush, lightly brush a sheet of phyllo dough with melted butter, then fold in half lengthwise. Place a salmon strip at one short end of the phyllo, about 1 inch from the edge of the bottom of the dough. Spread about 1 tablespoon of the tomato mixture over the salmon. Fold the short end of the phyllo over the salmon, then fold the bottom edge up and the top edge down, creating an envelope, and brush again with butter to seal the edges. Place on the baking sheet, seam side down. Repeat with the remaining phyllo, salmon, and tomatoes. (The phyllo envelopes can be prepared, covered, and refrigerated up to 4 hours ahead.)

3 Position a rack in the center of the oven and preheat to 450°F.

4 Brush the tops of the envelopes with reserved melted butter. Bake until the phyllo is golden brown, 12–15 minutes. Serve hot with a dab of hollandaise as a special treat, or serve cold, with a bit of homemade herbed mayonnaise or aioli.

Roasted Fall Vegetable Tart

This tart begins with a cheddar cheese crust that goes with almost any combination of fall vegetables. Here, it is filled with roasted leeks, fennel, and broccoli or Brussels sprouts. Beets or cauliflower would stand in beautifully, too. *Serves 6–8*

FILLING

2 leeks, white and pale-green parts only, rinsed and coarsely chopped

2 cups small broccoli florets or Brussels sprouts, trimmed and cut in half

2 small fennel bulbs, cleaned and thinly sliced lengthwise

1 small sweet red onion, sliced

1 tablespoon finely chopped fresh rosemary

½ teaspoon salt

¼ teaspoon freshly ground pepper

2 tablespoons extra virgin olive oil

1 whole head garlic, unpeeled

1 tablespoon sherry vinegar

⅓ cup Black Olive Tapenade (see facing page)

½ cup crumbled goat cheese

CRUST

1¼ cups white unbleached flour (or a mixture of whole-wheat)

½ cup cornmeal

1 cup shredded cheddar cheese

8 tablespoons (1 stick) cold unsalted butter, cut into small pieces

¼ cup yogurt or sour cream

1 Preheat the oven to 400°F.

2 Prepare the filling: Spread the leeks, broccoli or Brussels sprouts, fennel, and onion in a single layer on a large rimmed baking sheet. Season the vegetables with the rosemary, salt, and pepper. Drizzle the oil over the vegetables and toss to coat. Set the head of garlic in the corner of the pan. Bake, stirring occasionally, until the vegetables are tender when pierced with a knife and the garlic is soft, about 45 minutes. Remove from the oven, set aside the garlic, and douse the vegetables with the vinegar. Set aside to cool.

3 Lightly coat an 8-inch tart pan with olive oil, and reduce the oven temperature to 350°F.

4 Place the flour and cornmeal in a food processor. Pulse to combine. With the motor running, add the cheddar cheese, then the butter, one piece at a time, until incorporated. Add the yogurt and blend until the dough forms a ball. Transfer from the food processor onto a lightly floured surface. Knead gently with more flour as needed to form a ball, then press down with the palm of your hand. With a flour-dusted rolling pin, roll the dough into a shape to fit the tart pan, plus an extra inch around. Transfer to the tart pan and trim the overhang from the edges. (Can be made ahead to this point and refrigerated until ready to use.)

5 Spread the tapenade over the bottom of the crust. Top with the roasted vegetables. Cut the pointed top off the garlic, squeeze the roasted garlic onto the vegetables, and dot with goat cheese.

6 Bake the tart until the edges of the crust are golden brown, about 25 minutes. Let cool 5 minutes before removing the pan sides and cutting into squares.

Black Olive Tapenade

You can buy tapenade in a jar, or you can make your own. Here's how. *Makes 1 cup*

3 cups pitted kalamata olives

3 teaspoons extra virgin olive oil

3 teaspoons balsamic vinegar

2 cloves garlic

Combine all ingredients in a blender and mix for a few seconds, until smooth. The paste will be slightly granular.

Dessert for Dinner

Just when the leaves start to change in color from green to red and yellow, we change our culinary habits to start eating vegetables with red, yellow, and orange hues. In the fall, I am tempted to serve dessert for dinner. It's no secret that carrots, zucchini, winter squash, and apples can be turned into sweets with just a drizzle of apple cider or maple syrup.

Fill a pie crust with pumpkin, pecan, or apple filling and top with a scoop of pumpkin ice cream, and the meal is complete. Healthy desserts are a natural way to celebrate the harvest season, and it sure gets the kids to eat their vegetables.

Glazed Spiced Pecans with Brussels Sprouts

Brussels sprouts are at their best after a few hard, late-fall frosts. The cold weather smooths out the rough edges of their flavor and gives the sprouts a mellow sweetness. As a change of pace from buttered sprouts, this festive dish is perfect for a holiday dinner. *Serves 6*

½ cup pecans

4 tablespoons (½ stick) melted unsalted butter, divided

1 tablespoon sugar

½ teaspoon ground cumin

⅛ teaspoon cayenne pepper

1 pound Brussels sprouts, root ends trimmed, discolored leaves discarded, and a shallow X cut into the bottom of each sprout

Zest of 1 orange

Salt and freshly ground pepper, to taste

1 Preheat the oven to 400°F.

2 In a small bowl, toss the pecans with 1 tablespoon of the butter. Add the sugar, cumin, and cayenne pepper and stir to coat the pecans. Place the pecans in an even layer on a baking sheet and roast for 10 minutes, stirring occasionally, until fragrant. Set aside.

3 Meanwhile, bring a large pot of lightly salted water to a boil. Add the sprouts and cook until barely tender, about 8 minutes. Drain well. Return to the pot and toss with the remaining 3 tablespoons butter. Add the spiced nuts and toss to blend. Keep in a warm oven until ready to serve. Season with the orange zest, salt, and pepper.

Artichokes Stuffed with Herbed Bread Crumbs

This melt-in-your-mouth alternative to the classic steamed artichoke is tender and cheesy, and eliminates any requests for melted butter served on the side. This process is a bit more complicated than a simple steamed artichoke, but the result is worthwhile.   *Serves 4*

½ cup fine bread crumbs

½ cup freshly grated Parmigiano-Reggiano cheese

2 cloves garlic, minced

2 tablespoons chopped fresh mint

2 tablespoons chopped Italian flat-leaf parsley

1½ teaspoons coarse sea salt, divided

¼ teaspoon freshly ground pepper

½ cup extra virgin olive oil

4 large artichokes

1 In a food processor, combine the bread crumbs, cheese, garlic, mint, parsley, ½ teaspoon of the salt, and pepper and whir to finely chop the herbs and blend. Add the olive oil in a slow stream. Set the mixture aside.

2 With a sharp knife, cut the bottom stem off each artichoke so that it will sit flat. Trim off ½ inch from the top of each artichoke. With scissors, snip off the pointy tips from all the leaves. Gently spread open each layer of leaves and fill with the bread crumb mixture, using a spoon or your fingers to press the mixture inside the artichoke and distribute evenly. Dust the top with the remaining mixture, and press the leaves back together.

3 Place the artichokes in a heavy-bottomed saucepan that is just large enough to hold them snugly so they won't tip over. Add 1 inch water and the remaining teaspoon salt, and bring to a boil. Reduce the heat to low, cover the pot, and simmer for 30 minutes. Test for doneness by inserting a sharp knife through the center, or pull out a leaf and taste for tenderness.

4 Lift the artichokes from the pot with tongs and serve on individual plates (along with plenty of napkins). To eat, remove the leaves individually and, with your teeth, pull the meat from the leaf along with the seasoned bread crumbs. Reserve the cooking water and serve in a small dish on the side as extra dipping sauce.

The Patio Garden
Pot Luck

Garden Personality: *Not enough land for a garden? You can still follow this design and plant your favorite summer foods in pots. Create a sense of place that is defined by containers of ornamental edibles, ideal for the patio.*

Containers come in all sizes and shapes, and how you arrange the pots to fill the space will largely depend on the way your door opens onto the space or where the steps are located on or off the patio. Building the Patio Garden in layers will allow sunlight to reach all the plants. Place the larger pots in the back row; give them height by placing them on top of a tiered structure, with midsize pots in the middle rows and smaller plants dotting the front. If the pots are really large, position your containers on movable dollies before adding the soil and plants. Keep a watering can or hose nearby, and plan to keep the plants moist but not overwatered.

Give your plants ample room for their roots to expand, and feed them with good soil, which will ultimately affect their flavors. Not all soil is created equal, especially when it comes to potting soil blends; many are treated with a fertilizer infusion to boost plant growth. So read your ingredients label carefully, just as you would when selecting your own food at the grocery. Select organic blends with a mixture of natural compost; add peat or sand to lighten the soil, which will help the pots drain excess water, just in case you overwater from time to time. Each watering will leach nutrients from the soil, so plan on adding organic fertilizer to your watering can every two weeks or so, especially if the leaves start to turn purple or yellow, an indication of a nutrient deficiency.

In a Patio Garden, start with ample-sized plants rather than seeds. The result will be an instant garden, though the downside is that many mature plants will not last for a long season. Select plants that are specifically bred for containers, since these will be varieties that are more likely to remain compact and provide harvest.

Ten Tips for Growing a Patio Garden

1 The larger the pot, the less maintenance required. Smaller pots dry out easily and will need to be watered every day.

2 Most vegetable plants need 6 to 8 inches of soil to grow successfully. If your container is extra deep, insert several crushed empty plastic milk jugs to take up space.

3 Water in the morning and at midday, and keep plants watered daily. Be sure that adequate drainage is provided in the pots.

4 Do not reuse your potting soil each year, as it can contain soil-borne disease. Plan to empty it into your compost pile, and refill with fresh soil each year.

5 The flavor of your produce will be affected by the quality of your soil. Fill your containers with the best organic potting soil you can find, and blend in a handful of a slow-release organic fertilizer as needed throughout the season.

6 Before you bring home plants from a garden nursery, always check for white flies or aphids. If you find these on your plants, isolate them and treat them with an organic pest control such as soap spray.

7 Build a trellis for tomatoes, peas, and runner beans before they get too tall.

8 Interplant vegetables, flowers, and herbs in containers for beneficial companion planting.

9 Select plants that are bred to be grown in containers. Avoid space hogs, such as sweet corn and pumpkins, unless you have a lot of garden area.

10 Replant lettuce and other crops once you harvest, to maintain the garden's longevity.

OVERALL SIZE: *15 feet by 20 feet*
BED SIZE: *15 feet by 3 feet*
CENTRAL BED: *8 feet by 3 feet*
NUMBER OF BEDS: *3*
PATH WIDTH: *2 feet*
PATH MATERIAL: *Brick*

Patio Garden Plant List

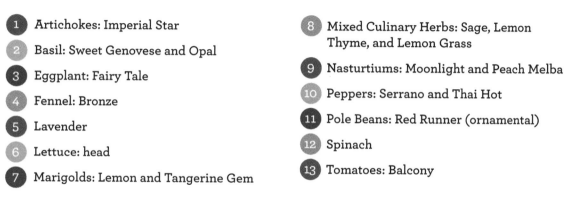

1. Artichokes: Imperial Star
2. Basil: Sweet Genovese and Opal
3. Eggplant: Fairy Tale
4. Fennel: Bronze
5. Lavender
6. Lettuce: head
7. Marigolds: Lemon and Tangerine Gem

8. Mixed Culinary Herbs: Sage, Lemon Thyme, and Lemon Grass
9. Nasturtiums: Moonlight and Peach Melba
10. Peppers: Serrano and Thai Hot
11. Pole Beans: Red Runner (ornamental)
12. Spinach
13. Tomatoes: Balcony

❸ Eggplant

The name eggplant derives from the fruits of some eighteenth-century European cultivars, which were yellow or white and resembled goose or hen's eggs. The plants have a spiny stem and white or pink flowers, producing fruit that can range from large round or oblong shapes to finger-size fruits. In areas where the growing season is short, start seeds indoors four weeks before transplanting to the garden in an area that gets full sun.

❺ Lavender

Most herb growers can never plant enough English lavender. It is the backbone of gardens throughout Europe, and with good reason. Its silvery foliage and aromatic purple blossoms attract bees and create a stunning border. Soil should not be overly rich; in fact, lavender prefers a dry, sandy soil. Since lavender is slow to germinate, it's best to purchase plants and transplant them into the garden. Favorites: Hidcote, Munstead, Lavender Lady.

❾ Nasturtiums

Trumpet-shaped and mildly spicy in flavor, nasturtiums are one of my favorite edible flowers. They adapt easily to growing in a pot, on a garden border, or up a trellis. The wide range of colors—from pale yellow to deep scarlet to brilliant orange—makes nasturtiums one of the most useful garden ornamentals. Leaves and flowers are both edible and can be added to salads or chopped into a seasoned butter for serving over cooked vegetables. Direct sow in the garden. Favorites: Alaska, Peach Melba, Empress of India, Whirlybird.

⑩ Peppers

Because of the wide variety of their shapes, sizes, and colors, peppers are some of the most interesting crops to grow in a kitchen garden. They prefer a warm climate and a long season, and since they are fruiting crops, be sure to enhance the soil and grow them alongside tomatoes and other crops that benefit from soil high in phosphorus. Sow in pots and transplant into the garden once the danger of frost is past.

⑫ Spinach

Spinach prefers the cool weather of early spring and late fall, and provides dark, leafy greens that are adaptable to many delicious recipes. Several types of spinach are available, consisting of smooth or crinkly leaves, and each will have a different degree of heat tolerance, so be sure to select the best match for your climate. The smooth leaves are best for salads, while the crinkly leaves are excellent served lightly steamed or in recipes. Direct sow seeds in the garden in prepared loose soil. Seeds can be planted tightly in a single row or broadcast in a block; allow 5 inches between rows in order to cultivate. Keep plants watered and harvest with scissors when leaves reach about 5 inches in height and before flower heads are formed. Favorites: Space, Regiment, Indian Summer.

Fennel Tomato Soup

Each spoonful of this French country-style soup delivers a warming taste of sun-ripened tomatoes. The lovage adds a hint of anise, which complements the fennel. Serve chilled to heighten the flavors.   *Serves 4 to 6*

4 ripe tomatoes

3 tablespoons extra virgin olive oil

2 leeks, trimmed, white parts coarsely chopped (about 2 cups)

1 carrot, coarsely chopped

1 rib lovage or celery, stem and leaves finely chopped

2 large cloves garlic, finely chopped

3 strips fresh orange zest, finely chopped

1 teaspoon finely chopped fresh thyme

1 fennel bulb, finely chopped

1 Turkish bay leaf

3 cups water

1½ cups vegetable broth

½ teaspoon salt

¼ teaspoon freshly ground black pepper

2 teaspoons chopped fresh Italian flat-leaf parsley

¼ cup chopped fresh basil

Pesto Croutons (see page 229)

1 Fill a large stockpot with water and bring to a boil.

2 Cut a shallow X in the bottom of each tomato with a sharp knife and drop into the boiling water for 10 seconds. Using a slotted spoon, transfer the tomatoes to a bowl of ice water and slip off the skins. Halve the tomatoes and squeeze gently over a bowl to extract the seeds and juices. Reserve the juice and chop the tomatoes.

3 Dry the stockpot; add the oil to the pot and heat over medium heat. Add the leeks, carrot, lovage, garlic, orange zest, thyme, fennel, and bay leaf. Stir until all the vegetables are softened, 5–8 minutes. Add the tomatoes, reserved juice, water, vegetable broth, salt, and pepper. Simmer, uncovered, for about 25 minutes, occasionally breaking up the tomatoes with a wooden spoon.

4 Taste and adjust seasoning. Discard the bay leaf and stir in the parsley and basil. Refrigerate until ready to serve. Garnish with pesto croutons.

Corn and Jalapeño Muffins

These pepper-dotted muffins have pockets of melted cheese and are ideal for serving with chili or black bean soup. Plant a wide variety of peppers, including jalapeño, habanero, serrano, Anaheim, and cayenne, as well as the tiny but incendiary Thai pepper, which is also an attractive indoor ornamental. A single hot pepper plant will produce a profusion of firecracker chilis. In this recipe, you can use any chili you have on hand, adjusting the amount to taste, as each pepper has a different heat level.   *Makes 12 muffins*

1 cup yellow cornmeal

1¼ cups unbleached all-purpose flour

½ cup whole-wheat flour

1 teaspoon baking powder

½ teaspoon baking soda

½ teaspoon sea salt

1 cup fresh corn kernels (cut from the cob)

1 cup milk

2 large eggs, beaten

6 tablespoons (¾ stick) unsalted butter, melted

½ cup grated cheddar cheese

1 jalapeño (or other pepper of your choice), cut into very thin ribbons

1 Position a rack in the center of the oven and preheat to 400°F. Lightly oil a 12-cup muffin tin with olive oil, or place a paper muffin sleeve in each cup.

2 In a medium bowl, mix together the cornmeal, flours, baking powder, baking soda, and salt. Make a well in the center, and add the corn, milk, and eggs. Stir the liquid mixture into the dry ingredients just until the ingredients are barely combined; the batter should still be lumpy. Add the butter and stir just until combined. Take care not to overmix or the muffins will not rise evenly and will have a dense texture.

3 Spoon a heaping tablespoon of the batter into each muffin cup. Sprinkle equal amounts of cheese and jalapeño over the batter in each cup. Spoon equal amounts of the remaining batter over each. Smooth the batter in each cup with the back of a spoon to be sure the batter covers the filling on the sides of the cup.

4 Bake until the muffins are golden brown, about 30 minutes. Cool in the pan for 5 minutes, then remove from the cups and serve hot.

Herb-Marinated Pork Tenderloin

The fragrance of this tender roast fills the house as it bakes, and it is an easy-to-prepare dish for a sit-down family meal. Serve it with a side of tasty homemade applesauce. *Serves 4*

½ cup mixed fresh herbs (thyme, rosemary, sage, chives)

¼ cup soy sauce

1 teaspoon ground ginger

3 cloves garlic, smashed

¼ cup olive oil

½ teaspoon salt

¼ teaspoon freshly ground pepper

1 (4- to 5-pound) boneless pork tenderloin

1 Strip the leaves from the stems of the herbs. In the bowl of a food processor, combine the herbs with the soy sauce, ginger, garlic, olive oil, salt, and pepper. Whir to blend.

2 Untie the roast from any strings or casing. Rub all over with the marinade—inside, outside, top, and bottom.

3 Place the roast in an ovenproof baking dish, loosely cover, and refrigerate for several hours. Return the roast to room temperature.

4 Preheat the oven to 350°F. Bake the roast for 1½ hours, or until the temperature is 165°F on an instant-read meat thermometer.

5 Remove the roast from the oven, cover with foil, and let sit for 15 minutes before carving.

Simple Homemade Applesauce *Makes 2 cups*

6 Macintosh or Jonagold apples, cored, peeled, and thinly sliced

¼ cup sugar

1 teaspoon cinnamon

¼ cup apple cider

In a saucepan, combine the apples with the sugar, cinnamon, and apple cider. Bring to a simmer and continue to cook, stirring occasionally, until gently stewed, about 10 minutes. Serve alongside oven-roasted pork, or on its own as a wholesome dessert, snack, or breakfast side dish.

Warm Spinach and Vermont Cheddar Custard

Cheddar and spinach are old friends, and are beautifully combined in this delicate custard. A lovely side dish, it would also make a fine brunch entrée. For a custard that is intensely rich in color and flavor, use farm-fresh eggs from free-range chickens. *Serves 4*

3 cups fresh spinach leaves, stems removed, and well rinsed

1 cup heavy cream

4 large egg yolks

1 cup shredded sharp cheddar cheese

¼ teaspoon sea salt

⅛ teaspoon freshly ground pepper

⅛ teaspoon freshly grated nutmeg

1 Position a rack in the center of the oven and preheat to 325°F. Lightly butter four 4-ounce ramekins.

2 Bring a large pot of lightly salted water to a boil. Add the spinach and cook until tender, about 3 minutes. Drain and rinse under cold water. A handful at a time, squeeze out the excess moisture from the spinach. Chop coarsely. You should have about 1 cup chopped spinach.

3 In a medium bowl, whisk the cream and yolks until well combined. Stir in the spinach, cheese, salt, pepper, and nutmeg. Ladle or pour equal quantities of the custard into the ramekins, and place them in a large roasting pan. Add enough hot water to come halfway up the sides of the ramekins.

4 Bake until the custard is set when given a slight shake, about 25 minutes. Let stand for 5 minutes. Run a knife around the inside of each ramekin and invert to unmold.

Eggplant Caponata

The secret to this delicious caponata is the roasted vegetable mixture with a sweet-sour accent of balsamic vinegar. For a Mediterranean-style lunch, heap the finished caponata on lettuce leaves and serve with a platter of assorted cheeses and lots of grilled crusty bread or crackers. It also doubles as a great vegetarian sandwich spread or a side dish with grilled fish.   *Serves 8*

1 medium eggplant, peeled and cut into ¾-inch cubes

4 each medium zucchini and summer squash, cut into ¼-inch-thick rounds

2 medium celery ribs, cut into ½-inch dice

1 large red onion, cut into ½-inch dice

1 large red bell pepper, seeded, ribbed, and cut into ½-inch dice

½ cup olive oil, as needed

3 cloves garlic, crushed under a heavy knife

1 teaspoon fine sea salt, plus more to taste

½ teaspoon freshly ground pepper, plus more to taste

½ cup balsamic vinegar, plus more to taste

¼ cup coarsely chopped pitted oil-cured black olives

¼ cup coarsely chopped pitted green olives, preferably Sicilian

¼ cup tomato paste

3 tablespoons capers, drained and rinsed

1 tablespoon finely chopped fresh oregano

Basil sprig and nasturtium flowers, for garnish

1 Position racks in the top third and center of the oven and preheat to 400°F. Lightly oil a large roasting pan. Spread the eggplant, zucchini, summer squash, celery, onion, and bell pepper in the roasting pan. Mix the oil and garlic and drizzle over the vegetables.

2 Season the vegetables with 1 teaspoon salt and ½ teaspoon pepper. Bake, stirring occasionally, until the vegetables are barely tender, about 30 minutes.

3 Whisk the vinegar, olives, tomato paste, capers, and oregano in a large bowl to dissolve the tomato paste, then pour over the roasted vegetables. Continue to bake, stirring occasionally, until the vegetables are tender, about 30 minutes. Season with salt and pepper and a dash of balsamic vinegar. Cool completely.

4 Garnish with a sprig of basil and nasturtium flowers.

Apple Crisp with Almond Topping

It makes perfect sense to eat dessert for dinner, if it is as healthy as this apple crisp. There are many variations of apple crisp, and this one with a nutty almond topping is different from my mom's. She makes hers with McIntosh apples, a traditional New England variety, but I prefer a firmer apple that will not turn into applesauce when it is baked.   *Makes one 10-inch pie*

FILLING

6 large Macoun or Cortland apples

1 teaspoon ground cinnamon

½ teaspoon ground ginger

⅛ cup Frangelico or amaretto liqueur

½ teaspoon vanilla extract

TOPPING

1 cup unbleached all-purpose flour

¾ cup sliced almonds, toasted in a 400°F oven until lightly golden-brown

½ cup granulated sugar

½ cup packed dark brown sugar

½ teaspoon salt

8 tablespoons (1 stick) unsalted butter

½ teaspoon pure almond extract

1 Position a rack in the center of the oven and preheat to 325°F.

2 Lightly butter a deep pie dish. Toss together the apples, cinnamon, ginger, liqueur, and vanilla. Spread evenly in the dish.

3 In the bowl of a food processor, mix together the flour, almonds, granulated sugar, brown sugar, and salt. Add the butter and almond extract, and pulse until crumbly. (This can also be done by hand in a mixing bowl, cutting with a pastry blender or fork.) Sprinkle the topping over the apples to cover, pressing gently.

4 Bake the crisp until the topping is golden and crisp and the apples are tender, about 1 hour. Serve with vanilla ice cream.

The Heirloom Maze Garden
Kokopelli's Labyrinth

Garden Personality: *Inspiration for the Heirloom Maze Garden comes from ancient labyrinths, circular paths that served as meditation retreats or offered an adventure with a surprise at the end. Follow a winding path past tall tomato teepees and archways of runner beans that leads to the center of the garden. Immerse yourself in the greenery that surrounds you and connect to the history of your heirloom open-pollinated plants.*

This garden is a far simpler version of a traditional maze, yet can be easily adapted to accommodate additional winding paths and taller plants. Building this garden may take a bit more patience and ingenuity than simply measuring out the four corners of a more traditional square garden. Plan to use a measuring tape, garden stakes, and lots of string to measure the perimeter and the pathways. Once you have the stakes and the string in place, take a walk to be sure that you have the dimensions exactly the way you want them before digging. If you have room to expand, increase the outer edges of this design and add an additional loop in the center.

Many garden plants love to grow vertically, and this maze design provides the perfect opportunity to establish a string of tall teepees to support a living wall of heirloom tomatoes, cucumbers, and pole beans. There are two ways that you can build a trellis to accommodate tomatoes and runner beans; either create individual teepees by lashing together three 8-foot poles at the top with garden twine, or set up a series of double poles that form an X. Run a 6-foot length across the top. Plant seeds in rows underneath the poles, and train seedlings to grow up a string until they reach the top. Build the understory with low-hugging plants such as summer squash, and dot the middle with fragrant sweet herbs and plants that thrive in a bit of shade, such as salad greens or flowers.

Heirlooms were grown before the introduction of hybrid plants in the 1950s, and for many years heirlooms were thought to be inferior in production and resistance to disease. There are many reasons to grow heirlooms over hybrids—better flavor, reliable productivity, and beauty—and one of their greatest assets are their seeds. When you grow heirloom plants, you are preserving agricultural history through open-pollinated plants, which offer the opportunity to harvest the seeds at the end of the season. Keep seeds in a cool, dry location and you can plant them again for next year's garden, as well as pass them along to friends. For an educational element, mark each of your plants with its origins, and maybe even install a small sign to share the history of your plants.

Don't try to tame this garden; instead allow it to grow wild. The Heirloom Maze provides a new perspective on vegetable gardens, from the inside out. Surround yourself in a totally green environment that envelops you as you enter; when the world ceases to satisfy, there is always the garden.

Ten Tips for Growing an Heirloom Maze Garden

1 Set out the design with stakes and string, then mulch the path with straw to give you a good idea of the size and shape of the garden.

2 Dig the beds and add additional compost and other soil amendments to be sure the beds are richly fortified to give the plants a boost.

3 Install the trellis before you plant; this will provide infrastructure.

4 Plant taller plants on north side, to allow southern sun to penetrate to shorter plants in the center.

5 Get a jump on the season with big plants, and start seeds indoors or purchase plants that are already growing.

6 If you have room, place a bench or a rock in the center for sitting to enjoy the greenery and the peace within.

7 If you enjoy entertaining outdoors, expand the size of the garden and plan to include a fire pit in the center.

8 Research heirloom plants and select varieties indigenous to your area. Label each plant to share the history of the varieties with others.

9 Allow a few of the plants to go to seed, and harvest the seeds for sowing the following season.

10 Use 8-foot bamboo poles for the trellis. Keep the trellis natural or paint it in wild colors for a touch of whimsy.

OVERALL SIZE: *18 feet by 18 feet*
OUTSIDE BED SIZE: *3 feet*
INSIDE BED SIZE: *3 feet by 4 feet*
PATH WIDTH: *2 feet*
PATH MATERIAL: *Bark mulch, straw, or grass*

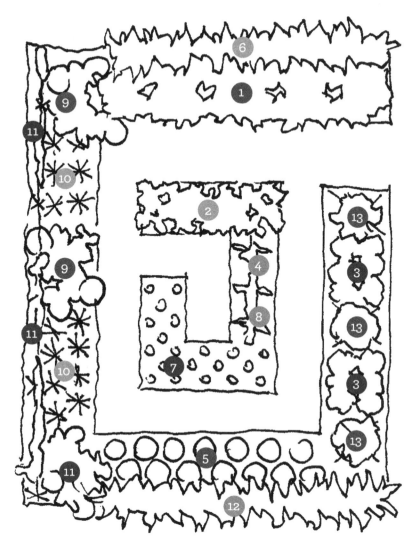

Heirloom Maze Garden Plant List

1. Beans: Lima Fordhook
2. Bean Shelling: Tongues of Fire
3. Broccoli: Spring Raab
4. Carrots: Parmex
5. Cabbage: Green and Red
6. Cucumber: Lemon
7. Endive: Chicory

8. Fennel: Zefa Fino
9. Melons: Moon and Stars
10. Onions: Top-Setting Walking
11. Peas: Green Arrow
12. Sunflowers: Velvet Queen
13. Tomatoes: Big Rainbow, Persimmon, Garden Peach, and San Marzano

 ## Beans

Sometimes gardening requires making tough choices—when it comes to planting pole beans or bush beans, I vote in favor of both! Plant pole beans on a trellis and you will find that the succulent beans are easy to spot and to harvest without bending down. Bush beans are tidy, compact plants, and are reasonably self-sufficient at staying healthy and out of trouble. Sow one seed about 1 inch deep, planting every 5 inches in a row or at the base of a trellis. Water, and seedlings should emerge within five to seven days. Flowers will appear, and beans will follow. If you are growing Filet Haricot Beans, these pencil-thin beans are best when plucked every other day or they will become thick and fibrous. Pole bean favorites: Trionfo Violetto Purple, Kwintus, Blauhilde, Borlotti. Bush bean favorites: Fin de Bagnols, Nickel, Royal Burgundy, Roc d'Or, Blue Lake.

⑥ Cucumbers

There are plenty of good reasons to grow cucumbers in a kitchen garden. They blend so well with other summer foods—chopped into salads, marinated in vinegar and sugar, or pickled with dill. Plan to grow them vertically on a trellis, where they will take up less room than sprawling on the ground. Direct sow in the garden or start in pots and transplant. Favorites: Lemon Cucumber, Diva, Suyo Long.

7 Endive: Chicory

Italians love their bitter greens, and for good reason. They are an excellent tonic to balance rich foods, as well as a natural source of iron. Chicory, dandelion, and frisee derive from wild plants, but can also be cultivated in the garden. Sow seeds directly in the garden in the spring or fall, and they will provide an ample source of greens year round. Plan to sauté them with a bit of bacon, or dress them with creamy vinaigrette to tame their bite. Favorites: Bianca Riccia, Clio Dandelion, Red Rib Dandelion, Catalogna, Witloof.

10 Walking Onions

The weight of the top-setting bulbs bends the stalks, allowing the bulblets to take root—hence the name. These novelty onions will creep across the garden—okay, not the most practical plant for a kitchen garden, but the top knot of bulblets is edible as well as ornamental.

13 Heirloom Tomatoes

The real secret to a delectable tomato is selecting the best variety. That's why I choose heirloom varieties, which are prized for their quirky colors, shapes, and depth of flavor. Start seeds in individual small pots four to six weeks before frost-free date and transplant when temperatures are safely above freezing. Keep plants trimmed to just the branches that have fruit. Favorites: Sun Gold Cherry, Red or Green Zebra, Persimmon, Big Rainbow, Garden Peach, Brandywine.

Chilled Lemon Cucumber Soup

Round, bright-yellow lemon cucumbers are a real treat to eat right off the vine. In a bumper-crop year, the plants are so abundant that a good soup recipe is needed to make a dent in the harvest. Standard cucumbers will work just as well in this refreshing chilled soup; it does not involve cooking, so it's ideal for hot days. *Serves 6*

6 lemon cucumbers or 2 large cucumbers

3 cups yogurt

1 fennel bulb, trimmed, fronds removed, and chopped

2 scallions, trimmed

2 eggs, hard-boiled

¼ cup pecans, dry roasted

1 tablespoon chopped fresh dill

1 tablespoon chopped fresh mint

1 tablespoon chopped fresh Italian flat-leaf parsley

1 tablespoon olive oil

Salt and pepper, to taste

Fennel fronds, for garnish

Nigella blossoms, or other edible flowers, for garnish

1 In batches, purée the cucumbers, yogurt, fennel, scallion, eggs, pecans, dill, mint, parsley, and oil in a blender or food processor.

2 Transfer to a bowl, cover, and refrigerate until chilled, at least 2 hours. Season with salt and pepper. Serve chilled, garnished with fronds of fennel and a single nigella blossom in each bowl.

Borlotti Bean and Kale Soup

Colorful dry beans may look great in glass jars, but when you have them growing fresh in the garden, it's time to make soup. Borlotti are the famous Lamon beans that make Italian soups so hearty and are the foundation of the classic pasta e fagioli. Speckled with red and white streaks, they are much like a cranberry bean, which can be substituted. Cooking with fresh beans means there is no soaking overnight, as you would have to do with dry beans, and in this soup they absorb the natural smoky bacon flavor and turn tender and juicy. Kale can be replaced with broccoli or savoy cabbage—or use all three, for a truly hearty vegetable combination. *Serves 4*

4 slices bacon, chopped into
½-inch pieces

2 medium leeks, white and pale-green
parts only, coarsely chopped

1 small butternut squash, peeled
and cubed into ½-inch pieces
(about 2 cups)

1 cup fresh shelling beans, such as
Borlotti or cranberry

1 head roasted garlic, squeezed to
remove soft pulp

2 sprigs fresh thyme

1 small sprig fresh rosemary

1 bay leaf

6 cups vegetable broth

2 cups chopped kale (or broccoli, or
savoy cabbage, or combine all three)

Salt and freshly ground pepper, to taste

Fresh Parmesan cheese, for garnish

Fresh flat-leaf Italian parsley,
for garnish

1 Cook the bacon in a large stockpot over medium heat, until golden and crisp. Drain the grease until only 2 tablespoons remain in the pot. Add the leeks to the bacon and sauté over medium heat until soft and transparent, 6–8 minutes.

2 Stir in the squash, beans, garlic pulp, thyme, rosemary, and bay leaf, and pour in the vegetable broth. Bring to a boil; reduce heat and simmer for 30 minutes, until the beans are tender. Halfway through cooking, add the kale. Remove the herbs and the bay leaf. Season with salt and pepper.

3 Pour half the mixture into a blender or food processor and blend until smooth. Stir the mixture back into the pot (this will create a smooth-and-chunky soup). Reheat to the desired temperature, if necessary. Garnish with the cheese and parsley and serve.

Corn, Cucumber, and Cilantro Salad

This cool, refreshing salad has the consistency of chunky salsa, but without the heat. Top-notch summer corn will supply plenty of sweetness with the sugar. For an extra depth of flavor, cook the whole corn on a grill instead of in boiling water, and then remove the kernels for the salad.
Serves 4 to 6

6 large ears fresh corn on the cob

2 large ripe tomatoes, seeded and chopped into ½-inch cubes

1 medium cucumber, chopped into ½-inch cubes

1 small sweet red onion, finely chopped

⅓ cup finely chopped fresh Italian flat-leaf parsley

½ cup finely chopped fresh cilantro

1 lemon, juiced (about 2 tablespoons)

3 tablespoons Maple Balsamic Vinaigrette (see page 49), or more to taste

Salt and freshly ground pepper, to taste

1 head butterhead lettuce

1 Cut each ear of corn in half and stand on its end to cut off the kernels. This should yield about 3 cups.

2 Drop the kernels into boiling salted water, and bring back to a boil. Turn off the heat, let stand for 1 minute, then drain in a colander.

3 Combine the corn, tomatoes, cucumber, onion, parsley, and cilantro in a large bowl. Add the lemon juice and toss. Toss with the vinaigrette, using more if you like. Season with salt and pepper.

4 Cover and refrigerate until chilled, at least 2 hours or overnight. Serve, chilled, atop the lettuce.

Fire-Roasted Tomato Sauce

Once you've tasted the intensity of a fire-roasted tomato sauce, it will become second nature to fire up the grill and prepare the tomatoes. The depth of flavor is perceptible, making this simple sauce the finest topping for pasta or pizza. Make up a big batch and store it in the refrigerator for up to a week, or in the freezer for several months. *Makes 2½ cups*

6 ripe but firm garden tomatoes,
   cut crosswise, with seeds removed

1 tablespoon extra virgin olive oil

1 medium onion, chopped

2 cloves garlic, minced

1 medium red pepper, roasted

½ cup chopped fresh basil

2 tablespoons chopped fresh thyme

1 bay leaf

Salt and freshly ground pepper,
   to taste

1 Build a fire in a charcoal grill and let it burn until the coals are covered with white ash. Place the tomatoes skin side down on the grill. Cook until the skins are blackened, about 3 minutes. Cool slightly and peel the skin from the tomatoes. Finely chop half the tomatoes and purée the remaining tomatoes in a blender or food processor.

2 Heat the oil in a large skillet over medium heat. Add the onion and garlic. Cook, un-covered, stirring often, until the onion is translucent, about 5 minutes. Add the puréed tomatoes, red pepper, basil, thyme, and bay leaf and bring to a simmer. Reduce heat to low and simmer, uncovered, until the sauce is reduced and thickened, about 15 minutes. Season with salt and pepper.

3 Serve hot over pasta, topped with grated Parmesan cheese, or on an herbed pizza crust as a base topping.

Braised Winter Greens with Coconut and Curry

This recipe is a one-stop approach to cooking winter greens like collards and kale, while maintaining their supremely vitamin-rich qualities. Turn this into a meal by adding cubed butternut squash and other fall-harvested vegetables. *Serves 4*

2 pounds collards, kale, or other winter greens

3 tablespoons olive oil

1 medium onion, minced (about 1 cup)

2 medium cloves garlic, minced or pressed

2 teaspoons grated fresh ginger root

1 teaspoon curry powder

1 cup chicken broth

1 (14-ounce) can light coconut milk

⅓ cup cashews

Juice of 1 lime

Salt and freshly ground pepper, to taste

1 Remove the ribs from the collards, and roll the leaves together to coarsely chop into 3-inch pieces. Finely chop kale leaves, if using. You should have about 6 cups. Rinse the leaves in a colander and drip-dry.

2 In a large, heavy-bottomed skillet or cast-iron Dutch oven, heat 2 tablespoons olive oil over medium heat. Add the onion and cook, stirring frequently, until softened and beginning to brown, about 5 minutes. Add the garlic, ginger, and curry; cook another 2 minutes.

3 Add half the greens to the skillet, with water still clinging to the leaves, and stir until they are beginning to wilt, about 1 minute. Add the remaining greens, the broth, and the co-conut milk. Cover the pot. Reduce the heat to medium-low and cook, stirring occasionally, until the greens are tender, about 15 minutes.

4 Meanwhile, place the cashews in a dry skillet over medium heat. Stir until lightly toasted, about 4 minutes. Coarsely chop and set aside.

5 Uncover the skillet and increase the heat to medium-high. Cook, stirring occasionally, until most of the liquid has evaporated and the greens begin to sizzle. Remove from the heat. Stir in the lime juice, the remaining tablespoon olive oil, and the cashews. Season with salt and pepper.

Roasted Carrots with Cippolini Onions

Because carrots are at the height of their flavor and nutritional value when pulled straight from the garden, it makes sense to grow your own. Round carrots are fun for kids to grow and ideal for gardens with heavier soil, since the roots don't have to sink very far. When you cook the carrots, keep about 1 inch of the tops attached; not only are they beautiful, but they are also proof that they were homegrown, with TLC. *Serves 4*

1 pound (about 8) young carrots, peeled, with tops

1 pound (about 16) small cippolini onions, trimmed

1 fennel bulb, top removed, thinly sliced

1 cup water

4 tablespoons (½ stick) unsalted butter

1 teaspoon sugar

1 tablespoon finely chopped fresh tarragon

½ teaspoon sea salt

1 Trim the tops off the carrots, leaving 1 inch of the green. Place the carrots, onions, and fennel in a medium saucepan with the water. Cover tightly and bring to a boil over high heat. Reduce the heat to medium-low and simmer for 5 minutes. Drain the water. Pat the vegetables dry, and slip the papery skin off the onions.

2 Preheat the oven to 375°F.

3 Melt the butter in a saucepan over medium heat; add the sugar, tarragon, and salt. Roll the carrots, onions, and fennel in the pan and sauté for 5 minutes, allowing them to lightly brown. Transfer to an ovenproof dish, and bake until tender and golden brown, about 10 minutes.

The Garnish Garden
Edible Flowers

Garden Personality: *Flowers bring an unmistakable aura to a garden. Edible plants grown in this garden go far beyond simple sprigs of parsley. Plant a full spectrum of colors, shapes, and flavors that showcase the best of edible flowers, which can double as bouquets for the table or garnish for the plate.*

nspiration for this garden comes from my neighbor Annie, who floats into the garden like a butterfly, touching each flower as if it were nectar for her soul. Her kitchen garden always stirs with magic; it is filled with a poetic blend of flowers and vegetables, a combination of squares and half-moons enclosed by a rim of sunflowers and a hedge of raspberries. She collects unusual flower vases to fill every room with bouquets, bringing the garden into the house. Annie taught me the value of taking time to appreciate the small nuances that a garden brings to the gardener, whether it is attracting honeybees or watching a darting hummingbird.

Annuals respond to frequent cutting, so plan to harvest your flowers and be rewarded with lush, bushy growth. Mixing ornamental vegetables with edible flowers in your Garnish Garden brings the best of both worlds together. Select vegetables that blend well with the flowers and that have longevity, so there are no gaps when the vegetables are harvested. Flowers have a way of transforming the garden—and any meal—into a work of art, and the Garnish Garden inspires the cook with a cascade of captivating blossoms.

Lay out the garden by building the outer squares first, and then measure in to the center circle. Edge the garden with a solid mass of low-growing greenery that will allow the garden to be viewed from all angles. Plan to start seeds in plug pots, and then transplant them into the garden. Allow adequate space between rows for the flowers to fully develop into bushy, robust plants. Make the paths of grass, to set off the colors of the garden and keep it looking natural.

Flowers and vegetables are equal partners in my garden, and the bouquets on the table also decorate the plate. From years of growing and tasting different varieties, I've developed a few favorites, and nasturtiums top my list. Blazing with peppery hot colors and spicy flavor, these brightly colored annuals originated in Peru and are commonly called Indian cress. The pungently flavored blossoms and the green lilypad-shaped leaves can be used in salads and are also reputed to have exceptional antioxidant qualities. There is something totally captivating about a brilliant blue blossom of borage adorning tomato soup, or a simple yet stunning viola scattered among thinly sliced cucumbers or a fruit salad. It is humbling to remember that eating flowers is nothing new. After all, bees have known all along how good flowers can be; now it's our turn.

Ten Tips for Growing a Garnish Garden

1 Start tender flowers indoors and transplant them into the garden after any danger of frost.

2 Harvest flowers early in the morning with clean scissors; take a vase of water into the garden with you.

3 Gently immerse edible flowers in cool water to release insects before garnishing your plates or salads.

4 Flower stems are like straws; they bring water up to the flowers. Recut the stems and change the water every few days.

5 When placing flowers in a vase, keep the arrangement loose and airy, allowing enough free space to allow a butterfly to fly freely in between stems.

6 To encourage new flowers, harvest frequently, just above the new leaf nodule.

7 Experiment with different varieties of edible flowers each season to keep expanding your repertoire.

8 Not all flowers are edible, and not all edibles are tasty.

9 For large blossoms such as calendula, rose, and chive, separate the petals from the flower heads before decorating salads.

10 Decorate the entrance of the Garnish Garden with an arbor covered with climbing roses or ornamental pole beans.

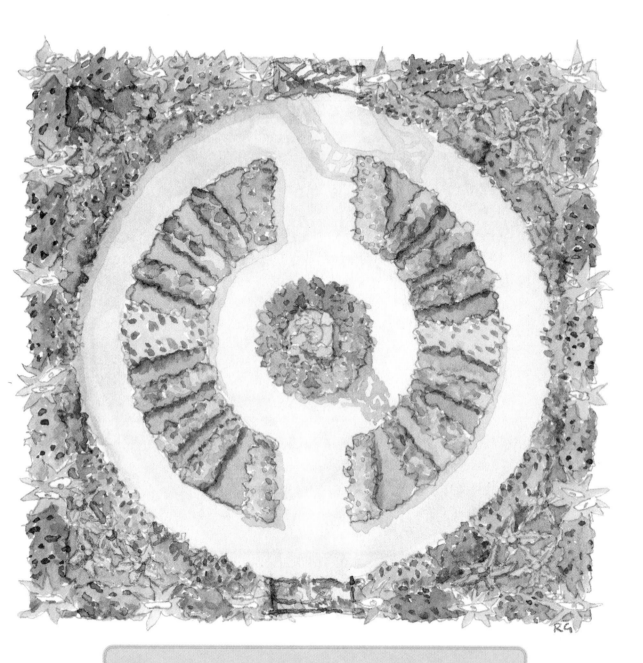

OVERALL SIZE: *15 feet by 15 feet*
INNER BED SIZE: *2 feet by 6 feet*
OUTER BED SIZE: *15 feet long/with cut out*
PATH WIDTH: *2 feet*
PATH MATERIAL: *Sod or bark mulch*

Garnish Garden Plant List

1. Artichokes: Imperial Star
2. Anise: Hyssop
3. Beans: Hyacinth Bean
4. Borage
5. Calendula: Flashback
6. Carthamus (Safflower): Zanzibar
7. Eucalyptus: Silver Dollar

8. Grass: Jester Ornamental and Silver Tip Wheat
9. Marigolds: Lemon Gem
10. Nasturtiums: Jewel Mix
11. Nigella: Love in a Mist
12. Salvia: Coral Nymph
13. Sunflowers: Italian White
14. Viola: Sorbet Formula Mix

Edible flowers top my list of must-haves in a kitchen garden. Most are easy to start from seed, either directly in the garden or indoors, and transplanted once the danger of frost is past. They can be used as garnish, or their petals can be sprinkled over a salad. They attract honeybees, hummingbirds, and other beneficial insects, and the colors of edible flowers contrast nicely with the green foliage of most vegetable plants. Favorites: Monarda, Calendula, Marigold, Nasturtium, Nigella, Hyacinth Bean, Lavender, Pansy, Sunflower, Hollyhock.

④ Borage

Also known as a starflower, borage is naturalized throughout the Mediterranean region, and grows to a height of 2 to 3 feet. Its stems and leaves are bristly, yet the brilliant blue blossoms are magnificent: five narrow, triangular petals with a flavor reminiscent of cucumber. Easy to grow, sow seeds directly in the garden or start ahead with plants.

⑤ Calendula

The name calendula means the first day of the month, presumably because pot marigolds are in bloom at the start of most months of the year since they bloom quickly—less than 60 days from seed to blossom. The color ranges from bright yellows, reds, and oranges and are remarkably frost hardy. Plant in a sunny location with rich, well-drained soil. Harvest blossoms frequently to keep the plants blooming. Calendula have a spicy flavor and can be added to salads and used as a garnish.

⑨ Marigolds

Tagetes tenuifolia is a single blossom marigold that is quite different than the common marigold. These ferny mounds of lemon-scented foliage provide a long blooming season for the kitchen gardener. They are ideal as an edging plant, though they will grow to 12 inches high, so keep them trimmed to maintain a compact plant. Start seeds indoors and transplant into prepared loose soil outdoors after danger of frost is past. Seeds can be direct sown, in a single row or broadcast in a block; allow 6 to 8 inches between rows in order to cultivate. Keep plants watered and harvest sprigs of flowers frequently to encourage growth. Favorites: Lemon Gem, Tangerine, Deep Red.

⑩ Nasturtiums

Trumpet-shaped and with a mild spicy flavor, nasturtiums are one of my favorite edible flowers in the garden. They adapt easily to growing in a pot, as a border, or up a trellis. The wide range of colors—from pale yellow to deep scarlet and brilliant orange—makes this one of the most useful garden ornamentals. Leaves and flowers are both edible and can be added to salads or chopped into a seasoned butter for serving over cooked vegetables. Direct sow in the garden. Favorites: Alaska, Peach Melba, Empress of India, Whirlybird.

Leek and Potato Soup

Leeks are easy to cultivate, but they do require a long growing season. This soup is one of the easiest to prepare, and it gets a colorful boost with the addition of fresh spinach leaves. *Serves 6*

4 tablespoons (½ stick) unsalted butter

4 medium leeks, white and pale-green parts only, coarsely chopped

2 cloves garlic

4 medium Yukon gold potatoes, cut into 1-inch cubes

6 cups chicken broth

½ teaspoon freshly grated nutmeg

1 bay leaf

1 packed cup coarsely chopped fresh spinach leaves

Salt and pepper, to taste

12 borage blossoms

1 In a large pot, heat the butter over medium-low heat. Add the leeks and garlic and cook, stirring, until the leeks are tender, about 15 minutes.

2 Add the potatoes and cook another 5 minutes. Add the broth, nutmeg, and bay leaf. Bring to a simmer over medium heat. Cover and simmer until the potatoes are tender, about 30 minutes. Remove the bay leaf.

3 With an immersion blender, purée the soup until smooth and creamy. Add the spinach leaves and pulse to blend.

4 Season with salt and pepper and garnish with several borage blossoms. Serve hot.

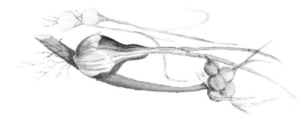

Arugula and Roasted Pear Salad

Arugula and pears flourish during the cooler late-autumn weather. Put them together for a great balance of sweet and piquant. The arugula is lightly dressed with a maple-sweetened vinaigrette to accentuate the natural flavor of the pears.   *Serves 4*

4 firm, almost-ripe pears (Bartlett or Bosc), peeled, cored, and cut lengthwise

2 tablespoons sugar

1 tablespoon butter, melted

2 tablespoons pine nuts

3 tablespoons olive oil

1 tablespoon balsamic vinegar

1 clove garlic, minced

Salt and pepper, to taste

½ teaspoon Dijon mustard

½ teaspoon maple syrup

6 cups arugula or mixed salad greens

2 tablespoons dried cranberries

¼ cup fresh Parmigiano-Reggiano cheese

12 calendula blossoms

1 Preheat the oven to 400°F.

2 In a medium bowl, toss the pears, sugar, and butter. Arrange the pears in a single layer on a baking sheet. Bake, turning once, until the pears are barely tender, 10–15 minutes.

3 Dry roast the pine nuts in a skillet for 5 minutes, until toasty brown. Remove from the heat and set aside.

4 In a large salad bowl, prepare the dressing by whisking together the oil, vinegar, garlic, salt, pepper, mustard, and maple syrup. Add the arugula or salad greens and toss to coat.

5 Divide the salad onto four chilled plates. Arrange the roasted pears in a fan around the center, and sprinkle with the cranberries, Parmesan cheese, and pine nuts. Scatter with petals from the calendula blossoms.

Spicy Mesclun with Herbed Cucumber Vinaigrette

If your goal is to taste your greens, count on this light and creamy dressing to balance the wild flavors of the more assertive greens often found in the fall. Puréeing vegetables into a salad dressing is a great way to give it body. The cucumbers provide a grassy flavor and a luxurious texture.

Serves 4

6 cups mixed mesclun greens

½ clove garlic

Pinch salt

¼ cup Herbed Cucumber Vinaigrette (see below), to taste

¼ cup dried cranberries

½ sweet red onion, thinly sliced

1 cup Baked Herb Croutons (see facing page)

12 viola blossoms

1 Wash and carefully dry the mesclun greens. Wrap them in a tea towel and refrigerate until ready to use.

2 Season a wooden salad bowl by rubbing with the garlic and salt. Add the greens; spoon over the dressing, to taste, and toss to coat. Add the cranberries, onion, and croutons, then toss again. Garnish with viola blossoms.

Herbed Cucumber Vinaigrette *Makes ¾ cup*

1 small cucumber, peeled, seeded, and chopped

¼ cup extra virgin olive oil

2 tablespoons red wine vinegar

2 tablespoons fresh chives

2 tablespoons fresh Italian flat-leaf parsley

1 tablespoon yogurt

1 teaspoon Dijon mustard

1 teaspoon Prepared Horseradish (see page 218)

1 teaspoon sugar

½ teaspoon salt

In a blender, purée all ingredients until smooth.

Asparagus with Lemon Chive Sauce

Homegrown asparagus spears are never uniform, so it's best to cook them lying flat in a skillet, removing the thinner spears as they become cooked. Any leftover creamy chive sauce can be used as a dip, sandwich spread, or sauce for grilled salmon. *Serves 4*

4 ounces cream cheese, at room temperature

¼ cup plain yogurt

Zest and juice of 1 lemon

2 tablespoons finely chopped fresh chives, divided

⅛ teaspoon ground cumin, dry roasted

⅛ teaspoon sugar

Salt and freshly ground pepper, to taste

12–15 spears asparagus (about 1 pound)

Blue borage flowers, for garnish

1 Prepare the sauce: In a medium bowl, mash the cream cheese and yogurt together until smooth. Whisk in the lemon juice and zest, 1 tablespoon of the chives, the cumin, and the sugar. Season with salt and pepper and set aside.

2 Snap off the tough stems of the asparagus. With a vegetable peeler, remove the tough skin from the thicker spears up to the bud.

3 Fill a large skillet halfway with lightly salted water and bring to a boil over high heat.

Add the asparagus spears, laying them flat in the water. Cook until the spears are just tender when pierced with the tip of a knife, 4–8 minutes, depending on their size. As the spears become tender, transfer them with tongs to a colander. Rinse the asparagus under cold water and drain well.

4 Arrange equal portions of the asparagus on salad plates and top with a spoonful of the sauce. Garnish with the remaining chives, and dot with blue borage flowers.

Baked Herb Croutons

1½ cups cubed whole-wheat or multigrain bread

⅛ cup olive oil

1 teaspoon chopped fresh rosemary

Preheat the oven to 375°F. In a bowl, toss together all the ingredients. Spread the bread cubes out in a single layer on a cookie sheet, and bake for 15 minutes, or until crispy, stirring to cook evenly. Remove from the oven and toss into the salad.

Arugula Pesto with Herbed Ricotta Gnocchi

There is something so satisfying about making gnocchi—tender pillows of dough that do not require a pasta machine. For the best result, use fresh ricotta (as opposed to commercial brands), which is available at local farmers' markets or cheese stores. The bright-green pesto proves that you don't have to use basil to get a terrific herb sauce for pasta. *Serves 4 to 6*

PESTO

2 cloves garlic, peeled and pressed

¼ cup pine nuts, toasted

1½ cups arugula leaves, well rinsed and towel-dried

1½ packed cups fresh spinach leaves, well rinsed and towel-dried

¼ cup freshly grated Parmesan cheese

½ cup olive oil

Salt and freshly ground pepper, to taste

GNOCCHI

1 cup semolina flour

1 tablespoon finely chopped fresh chives

1 tablespoon finely chopped fresh sage

1 tablespoon finely chopped fresh chervil

1 tablespoon finely chopped fresh fennel leaves

½ teaspoon fine sea salt

¼ teaspoon freshly ground nutmeg

¼ teaspoon freshly ground pepper

1 pound whole-milk ricotta cheese, drained

Olive oil, for tossing gnocchi

12 lemon gem marigolds

1 Make the pesto: With the motor running, drop the garlic through the feed tube of a food processor to mince. Add the pine nuts, arugula, spinach, and Parmesan and pulse until the greens are finely chopped. With the motor running, gradually add the oil to make a thick paste. Season with salt and pepper. Transfer to a small bowl and cover tightly with plastic wrap. (The pesto can be made up to 2 hours ahead and kept at room temperature.)

2 Make the gnocchi: Place the semolina, chives, sage, chervil, fennel, salt, nutmeg, and pepper in the bowl of a food processor and pulse to combine. Transfer to a medium bowl and, with your hands, blend in the ricotta. Flour your hands and knead the dough in the bowl until all the ingredients cling together. The dough will be sticky, but do not add more flour or the gnocchi will be heavy.

3 Line a baking sheet with waxed paper and dust with flour. Place about ⅓ cup of dough at a time on a lightly floured work surface and roll it underneath your palms to make a ½-inch-thick rope. Cut the rope into ¾-inch-long pieces. Using the tines of a fork, press an indentation into each piece and place the gnocchi on the baking sheet. Repeat until all the dough is used.

4 Bring a large pot of lightly salted water to a boil. Add the gnocchi and cook until they rise to the surface. Boil for 30 seconds, until the gnocchi are set but tender. Drain well. (The gnocchi can be made up to 4 hours ahead, rinsed under cold water and drained well.) Toss the gnocchi with olive oil and store at room temperature. To reheat, cook in a large nonstick skillet over low heat, or drop into boiling water to warm. Toss the hot gnocchi with the pesto, garnish with marigolds, and serve immediately.

List of Edible Flowers

Edible flowers make a wonderful garnish in a salad or soup or on a plate. Here are some of my favorites, which will add a splash of color and a quick burst of flavor:

Anise Hyssop	Chive	Pansy
Arugula	Cornflower	Rose
Bee Balm	Daylily	Snap Dragon
Borage	Herbs	Scented Geranium
Calendula	Marigold	Violas
Chamomile	Nasturtium	

The Chef's Garden
Herbs and Aromatics

Garden Personality: *With a strong focus on savory herbs and ornamental garnish, this garden provides a variety of options for the culinary professional seeking the ultimate fresh experience.*

One of the ways Chef Russell, executive chef at the Equinox Resort, shares his love of fresh ingredients is with a tour of his garden, located just outside the kitchen door. It's not a large garden, and he doesn't expect to supply the five restaurants at his exclusive hotel with the harvest. But he does enjoy teaching culinary students and guests how to identify basil, when to harvest rosemary and thyme, and the difference between tarragon and sage.

In early spring, Chef Russell finds time between meals to recruit his restaurant staff to prepare the soil, lay out the garden, and plant herbs, edible flowers, heirloom tomatoes, and hot peppers. He plants beans and broccoli, too, just to show the culinary students how these crops grow, and to build an appreciation for ingredients from the ground up. Guests at the hotel admire the garden as well, with a bird's-eye view down into the courtyard. Many chefs are learning that a kitchen garden goes beyond the mere cultivation of food. Teaching, eating, slowing down, avoiding chaos—these are all ways that a kitchen garden improves the busy lives of chefs. A Chef's Garden planted with herbs that can be used for fresh garnish, colorful peppers for decoration, and a row of heirloom tomatoes for a connection to the past can fulfill much the same purpose in your home.

Ten Tips for Growing a Chef's Garden

1 Select plants that you can't get from a lo-cal grower or crops that are not available from the farmers' market. (Avoid squash, corn, and other space hogs.)

2 Focus on culinary herbs and garnish plants that will enhance plate presenta-tion.

3 Start with plants instead of seeds for an instant garden that will have a quicker yield.

4 Extend the season with a hoop house or greenhouse for tomatoes and other ten-der crops.

5 Mark each plant with an ID tag, to give culinary students and other visitors an education.

6 Keep scissors and a washable harvest basket near the back door of your kitchen for easy access.

7 Install an outdoor sink as a separate washing area.

8 Provide wide paths for easy access to beds and plants.

9 Grow organically and do not use sprays or pesticides.

10 Support your local farms, and cultivate them as a resource.

OVERALL SIZE: *18 feet by 28 feet*
PERIMETER BEDS: *3 feet deep*
CENTER BEDS: *2½ feet by 8 feet*
CENER PATH WIDTH: *3 feet*
SIDE PATHS: *2 feet*
PATH MATERIAL: *Bark mulch*

The Chef's Garden Plant List

1. Basil: Red Rubin
2. Chives
3. Leeks
4. Lemon Verbena
5. Marigolds: Lemon Gem
6. Nasturtiums: Whirlybird

7. Parsley: Italian Flat-Leaf
8. Peppers: Hot Serrano and Jalapeño
9. Rosemary: Upright
10. Tarragon: French
11. Thyme: Lemon
12. Tomatoes: Cherry types (Yellow Pear and Sungold)

Basil

The basil family comprises close to eighty different types, although only about a dozen are used for culinary purposes. A tender annual, basil is easily started from seed or purchased as a plant; it thrives on heat and full sun. Start with a classic sweet basil, then add scented basil, reserving the miniature basil for a border plant. Start seeds indoors and transplant into prepared loose soil outdoors after the danger of frost is past. Or direct sow seeds into prepared soil, either in a single row or broadcast in a block; allow 6 to 8 inches between rows in order to cultivate. Favorites: Sweet Genovese, Fine Green, Red Rubin, Mammoth, Lemon, Cinnamon, Dark Opal, Thai.

③ Leeks

Tall, regal leeks look magnificent in your vegetable garden, and they are prized by chefs for their buttery flavor in soups and vegetable dishes. They are often expensive to buy, but they take little effort to grow, as they are relatively pest- and disease-proof. Dig a trench 4 to 6 inches deep and set your seedlings 6 inches apart. Backfill the trench until the tips of the plants are 2 inches above the soil. Favorites: King Richard, Lancelot, Blue Solaise.

⑧ Hot Peppers

Because of the wide variety of their shapes, sizes, and colors, peppers are some of the most interesting crops to grow in a kitchen garden. They prefer a warm climate and a long season, and since they are fruiting crops, be sure to enhance the soil and grow them alongside tomatoes and other crops that benefit from soil high in phosphorus. Sow in pots and transplant into the garden once the danger of frost is past.

12 Tomatoes

Tomatoes are the most popular garden plant, but they can easily take up excessive room in a compact kitchen garden. Build ornamental teepees with bamboo poles, or invest in rugged tomato cages to keep plants upright. Mulch the base with straw to keep the soil moist and the lower leaves from touching the soil. Focus on heirloom varieties that offer you a range of colors and flavors that go beyond the ordinary. The real secret to a delectable tomato is selecting a variety that suits your climate. Prestart seeds in individual small pots four to six weeks before the frost-free date and transplant when temperatures are steadily above freezing. Mulch the base of the plants with straw to prevent water from splashing soil onto the bottom leaves, which can cause soil-borne disease. Keep suckers trimmed to just the branches that have fruit. Favorites: Sun Gold Cherry, Red or Green Zebra, Persimmon, Big Rainbow, Garden Peach, Brandywine.

Golden Tomato Gazpacho with Basil

This unconventional gazpacho can be as spicy or mellow as you wish, depending on the amount of hot sauce you use. You can hand chop, or combine the ingredients in a food processor and whir until smooth. Chill, and serve garnished with croutons and edible flowers.   *Serves 4*

1 navel orange, peeled and cut into
　　1-inch pieces

4 medium yellow Persimmon tomatoes,
　　coarsely chopped (about 4 cups)

2 sweet bell peppers, coarsely chopped

1 cucumber, peeled and coarsely chopped

½ sweet onion, finely chopped

1 clove garlic, minced

¼ cup sweet basil leaves

¼ cup olive oil

¼ cup sherry vinegar

¼ teaspoon fiery hot sauce or Tabasco,
　　or more, to taste

Salt and papper, to taste

Lemon basil sprigs, for garnish (optional)

Pesto Croutons (see page 229, optional)

Crème fraîche, for garnish (optional)

1 Place orange, tomatoes, peppers, cucumber, onion and garlic in a blender. Pulse to coarsely chop. Add the basil, olive oil, sherry vinegar, and hot sauce, and pulse to blend, either until smooth or keep a few chunks for texture.

2 Cover and refrigerate until well chilled, at least 1 hour. Taste, and season with salt and pepper as desired. Serve the soup in chilled bowls, garnish with a sprig of lemon basil, pesto croutons, or a swirl of crème fraîche.

Spinach Salad with Warm Bacon Dressing

A warm dressing tenderizes spinach leaves and makes a timeless combination with a generous crumble of bacon, thinly sliced red onion, and soft chèvre. Parsley adds a nutritional wallop of vitamins C and K. *Serves 4*

6 strips thick bacon

½ cup plus 2 tablespoons extra virgin olive oil, divided

2 cloves garlic, minced

2 teaspoons honey

1 teaspoon Dijon mustard

Juice of 2 lemons (about 6 tablespoons)

¼ teaspoon salt

⅛ teaspoon ground pepper

1 shallot, minced

1 cup shiitake mushrooms, stems removed

8 cups fresh spinach, stemmed, washed, and dried

½ cup Italian flat-leaf parsley, chopped

½ sweet red onion, thinly sliced

2 ounces chèvre (goat cheese), softened

1 Preheat the oven to 375°F. Place the bacon on an ovenproof baking tray and bake for 20 minutes, turning once, until crisp. Transfer to a paper towel to drain excess grease, and set aside.

2 Combine ½ cup of the olive oil, garlic, honey, mustard, lemon juice, salt, and pepper in a small saucepan. Bring to a simmer, remove from the heat, and set aside.

3 Heat the remaining 2 tablespoons olive oil in a skillet. Add the shallot and mushrooms and sauté over medium-high heat, stirring frequently, until golden, 5–7 minutes.

4 Lower the heat to medium. Add the spinach to the sauté pan and gently toss, to slightly wilt the greens. Transfer the spinach mixture to a salad bowl, then add the parsley.

5 Pour the warm dressing over the spinach salad and toss well. Taste, and adjust seasoning as necessary. Coarsely crumble the cooked bacon, sliced onion, and softened goat cheese over the salad and serve.

Stewed Leeks with Fillet of Salmon

Redolent with creamy butter and sharp tarragon, these leeks get the royal treatment when served with simple grilled salmon. Slow-simmering leeks turn sweet and earthy, and they melt in your mouth. This will quickly become a favorite meal that can be prepared with ease for company or an intimate romantic dinner for two, served with a chilled Chardonnay. *Serves 4*

8 tablespoons (1 stick) unsalted butter, divided

5 tablespoons olive oil, divided

4 leeks, trimmed, cleaned, and chopped into ½-inch sections

Salt and freshly ground pepper, to taste

½ cup dry white wine

1 shallot, minced

3 tablespoons crème fraîche

1 tablespoon chopped fresh tarragon

1½ pounds wild salmon fillets, divided into 4 portions

Fresh chervil, finely chopped, for garnish

1 In a medium saucepan, melt 2 tablespoons of the butter with 2 tablespoons of the olive oil. Add the leeks and season with salt and pepper. Cover and simmer, stirring often, to soften and caramelize, about 20 minutes.

2 Meanwhile, cut the remaining butter into small pieces and set aside.

3 In a small saucepan, combine the wine and shallots and boil over medium-high heat until reduced by two-thirds, about 5 minutes. Reduce heat to low and whisk in the crème fraîche, then add the butter a piece at a time, whisking until smooth. Add the tarragon, cover, and keep warm.

4 Skin the salmon and lightly season with salt and pepper. In a large cast-iron skillet, heat the remaining oil over medium heat, and gently sauté the salmon, turning once, until cooked through, about 5 minutes per side.

5 To serve, divide the caramelized leeks among four plates. Spoon a generous amount of the sauce over the leeks, then place the salmon on top of each. Drizzle with more sauce and garnish with the chervil.

Glazed Vermont Quail

Quail makes a wonderful holiday dish, and is a good way to showcase other winter foods such as roasted potatoes and creamed kohlrabi.   *Serves 4*

4 boneless Vermont-raised quail (Vermont quail are small, and you may want to allow 2 birds per person)

Salt and freshly ground pepper, to taste

2 tablespoons olive oil, plus more if needed

2 tablespoons unsalted butter

2 shallots, minced

¼ cup finely chopped portobello mushrooms

1 teaspoon fresh sage

1 teaspoon fresh lemon thyme

½ cup dried cranberries, softened in boiling water and drained

1 cup plain bread crumbs

½ cup boiled cider, balsamic vinegar, or Marsala wine

1 Preheat the oven to 350°F.

2 Place the quail in a large bowl and season with salt and pepper.

3 In a large skillet, heat the oil and butter over medium heat. Add the shallots and sauté until softened. Add the mushrooms and herbs and sauté for 3–5 minutes, until gently cooked. Transfer to a bowl and stir in the cranberries. Add the bread crumbs, then toss to combine.

4 Place the quail on a cutting board or platter. With your hands or a spoon, loosely fill the cavities with the stuffing. Tie together the legs or make a slit in the skin and link one leg through to keep them together. Continue this for each of the quail.

5 Heat the skillet over medium heat, adding another tablespoon of oil if needed to keep the quail from sticking. Sauté the quail less than 1 minute on each side, turning to brown evenly. (The quail will puff up nicely.) Transfer to an ovenproof dish.

6 Deglaze the pan with the boiled cider, vinegar, or wine, and pour the glaze over the quail. Bake for 15 minutes. Serve warm.

Rainbow Beet Soufflé

This elegant soufflé, with sweet beets and a hint of orange, is so rich that I have considered serving it as a dessert. The crimson of the beets will bleed into the green-flecked yellow soufflé to create a beautiful rainbow effect. An assortment of colored beets such as chioggia, golden, and traditional red create an impressive array of colors. *Serves 4 to 6*

4 medium beets with greens

Olive oil for drizzling

Grated zest of 1 large orange

⅓ cup fresh orange juice

½ teaspoon sugar

½ teaspoon sea salt

⅛ teaspoon freshly ground pepper

4 tablespoons (½ stick) unsalted butter, softened

2 tablespoons freshly grated Parmesan cheese

½ cup crumbled goat cheese

3 tablespoons unbleached all-purpose flour

1 cup milk

4 large eggs, separated

1 Trim the tops off the beets, and place the tops in a medium saucepan with enough lightly salted water to cover. Bring to a boil and simmer until tender, about 2 minutes. Drain, rinse the beet tops under cold water, and coarsely chop. This should yield about ½ cup. Squeeze out the excess moisture, pat dry between paper towels, and set aside.

2 Preheat the oven to 400°F. Place the beets on a baking sheet, drizzle with a small amount of olive oil, and bake until the beets can be pierced with a knife, about 30 minutes depending on the size of the beet. Remove from the oven, cool, and slip off the skins. Slice into ⅛-inch-thick rounds and transfer to a medium bowl. Mix in the zest, juice, sugar, salt, and pepper.

3 Reduce the oven temperature to 375°F. Butter a 1-quart soufflé dish with 1 tablespoon of the butter. Sprinkle the bottom of the dish with the Parmesan cheese. Layer the sliced beets, with their juices, in the bottom of the dish, and then sprinkle with the goat cheese.

4 Prepare a béchamel sauce by gently melting the remaining 3 tablespoons butter in a medium saucepan over medium-low heat. Slowly whisk in the flour and let it cook without browning for a couple of minutes. Gradually whisk in the milk, whisking continuously until the sauce is thickened. Remove from the heat and cool slightly. Whisk in the egg yolks, one at a time, then gently fold in the cooked beet tops.

5 In a medium bowl, beat the egg whites until they form soft peaks. Gently stir the whites into the béchamel, then pour the sauce over the beets and place in the oven.

6 Bake until puffed and golden brown, about 30 minutes. Serve immediately.

Quick and Easy Cucumber Dill Pickles

Jars of homegrown pickles, jams, and relishes on the shelves are like money in the bank, and they bring a sense of pride. I make condiments starting in late summer through the fall, and offer this foolproof recipe for pickles as one of the easiest to get you started with canning. Be sure to read up on how to sterilize jars in a hot water bath and follow the proper procedure. *Makes 2 quart jars*

½ cup coarse kosher salt

16–20 small Kirby cucumbers, tips trimmed, well washed

1 tablespoon sugar

2 cups apple cider vinegar

12 black peppercorns

8 cloves garlic, peeled

1 bay leaf

1 bunch dill

2 horseradish or grape leaves

1 In a large bowl, dissolve ¼ cup of the salt in 2½ cups water. Add the cucumbers and set aside for 12 hours. Drain and rinse with cold water.

2 Combine the remaining ¼ cup salt, the sugar, vinegar, and 2 cups water in a saucepan. Bring to a boil. Add the peppercorns, garlic, and bay leaf and boil for 2 minutes.

3 Fit the cucumbers upright in 2 sterilized jars. Slice them in halves or quarters if necessary. Tuck in the dill.

4 Wipe the jar rims clean with a hot towel and screw on the sterilized lids. Immerse the jars in a hot water bath for 15 minutes, remove, and allow to cool on the counter. Label the jars and set on a shelf for a minimum of 3 months to allow the flavors to develop.

The Family Garden
Outdoor Fun

Garden Personality: *It's time to consider how a vegetable garden can be more than just a place to grow food. It can be a place to get the whole family involved and build connections essential for a lifelong appreciation of good, healthy food.*

 etting up a perfect dynamic between the stovetop, the sink, and the refrigerator forms the foundation of good kitchen design and saves you extra steps. Likewise, a well-designed Family Garden gives you freedom of movement; balancing the structures and the planting beds will result in a garden that is easy to maintain, hugely productive, and an outdoor living environment that the whole family will enjoy together.

You can begin the process of designing your Family Garden by asking basic questions: What does your family like to eat? What do they want to grow? How much time do you have for a garden? What elements would you enjoy in a garden that go beyond simple food production? Make a list of what tasks might engage your family that go beyond daily maintenance.

Plan to invest in good garden tools that will make your daily tasks more enjoyable. Be sure to select tools that are a good fit for the whole family; well-constructed child-size tools are a better investment than short-lived plastic toys. Add longevity to your garden season by making a long-term investment in perennial plants such as rhubarb, asparagus, fruit trees, blueberries, and strawberries. These can be planted around the perimeter of the garden or on the edges of the garden beds. Gardens are an investment in time and patience, but the rewards will be enjoyed year after year and be long remembered as time well spent by you and your family.

Ten Tips for Growing a Family Garden

1 Surround the garden with perennial flowers and enjoy color all season.

2 Build a garden shed for easy access to garden tools, and as a playhouse for kids.

3 Use only natural, untreated wood for the raised beds. Avoid using any chemically treated wood or plastic that will leach into your soil.

4 Plant sweet-smelling, night-blooming vines in pots near the picnic table.

5 Prepare paths that are easy to maintain and weed free, such as crushed gravel.

6 Slightly raised beds will give the garden area a distinct border.

7 Add a chicken house and a flock of hens to add an element of fun.

8 Make it easy for kids to graze in between meals; plant sugar snap peas, cherry tomatoes, and round carrots.

9 Locate compost piles outside the garden, with easy access through a gate.

10 Eat al fresco in the garden as often as possible.

Chickens

Every kitchen garden needs a flock of chickens to scratch around the paths looking for bugs or hang around the compost pile in search of kitchen scraps. If you can plan a nearby coop, you and your children will have fun checking for eggs and watching the chickens scurry for flying grasshoppers in the grass. Chicken yards are also a great place to toss discarded garden weeds; the chickens will happily eat them, and the compost can go back into the garden. And few kitchen staples are as essential as the egg.

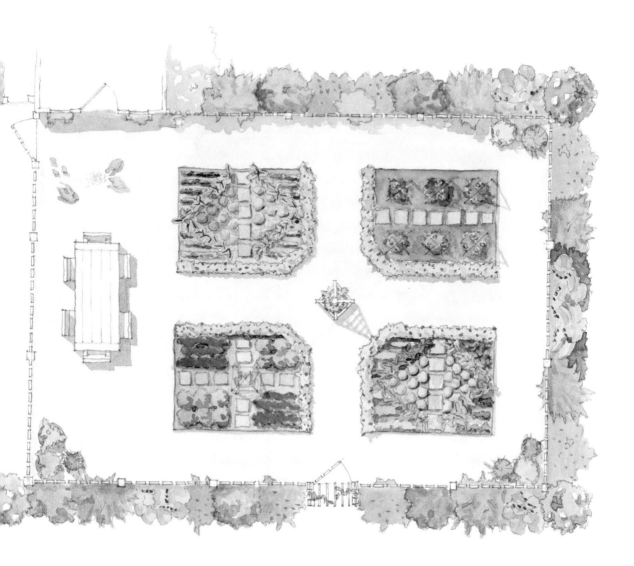

OVERALL SIZE: *40 feet by 24 feet*
BED SIZE: *8 feet by 12 feet*
PATH WIDTH: *4 feet*
BORDER: *5-foot perennial bed outside fence*
RAISED BED: *Rough hewn cedar or logs*
PATH MATERIAL: *Small pea stone*
FENCE: *White picket fence*

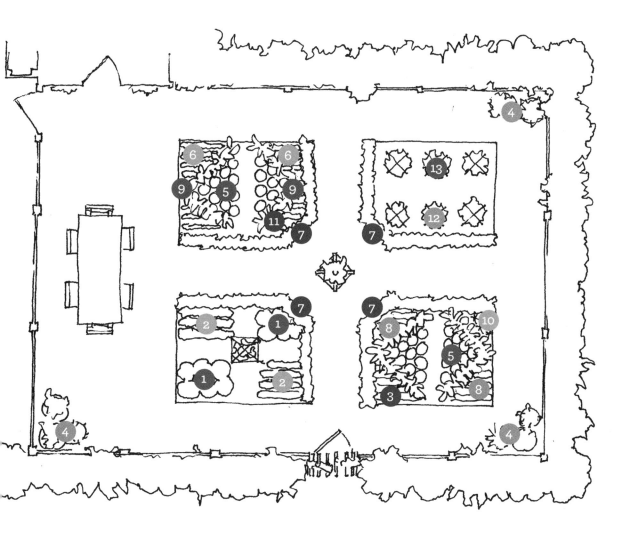

Family Garden Plant List

1. Basil: Sweet Genovese and Fino Verde
2. Beans: Triomphe de Farcy
3. Carrots: Touchon and Parmex
4. Herbs: mixed
5. Lettuce: Mixed Butterhead
6. Mesclun Mix: Provencal, Cutting Mix, Nicoise

7. Nasturtiums: Empress of India, Whirlybird, and Peach Melba
8. Onions: Shallots and Walla Walla
9. Peas: Sugar Snap
10. Peppers: Sweet Chocolate
11. Spinach: Indian Summer
12. Squash: summer and winter Butternut
13. Tomatoes: Persimmon and Peach

⑤ Lettuce

With over 150 different types of lettuce to choose from, you can select from a range of frilly, frosty, or compact heads of lettuce to paint into your garden landscape. Seeds can be direct sown in a single row or in a block; allow 6 inches between heads. For best results, start seeds in plug trays and transplant into the garden when 3 inches tall and a good root system is in place. Keep plants watered and harvest with scissors when heads are formed and before a seed shoot develops in the center, which makes the lettuce bitter in flavor. Lettuce seed does best in cool weather, and seed will not germinate in temperatures higher than 70°F. Favorites: Matchless, Four Seasons, Red Butterworth, Oliver, Little Gem, Red Grenoble, Craquerelle du Midi, Reine des Glaces, Oakleaf.

⑥ Mesclun

Mesclun makes it easy for salad lovers to harvest a range of greens from a single packet of seeds. Individual components of mesclun can be planted separately, and then combined together in the salad bowl. Direct sow seeds in the garden in prepared loose soil. Seeds can be planted tightly in a single row or broadcast in a block; allow 5 inches between rows in order to cultivate. Keep plants watered and harvest with scissors when 5 to 8 inches tall. For a cut-and-come-again crop, leave roots in the ground, and another crop will resprout. Favorites: Provencal, Misticanza, Nicoise.

8 Onions

Seeds can take a long time to germinate for some onion varieties, and it is advisable to start with either young plants or small bulblets, called sets. Onions are daylight-sensitive, so ideal varieties will depend on whether you are in the southern or northern hemisphere. Plant in the spring, and thin out the rows by harvesting young scallions during the summer. When the tops turn brown, and fall over, you will know the onion has stopped growing and will be ready to harvest from the ground. Favorites: Walla Walla, Vidalia, Rossa di Milano, Torpedo Red Bottle, Red or White Cippolini, Copra, Summer Bunching Scallions.

8 Shallot

If you've grown garlic, you'll be pleased to discover shallots, which take half the time to grow and are just as foolproof. They can be grown from either bulbs or seeds. The easiest strategy is to simply push the bulbs into the soil in the early spring. Leave about 6 inches between each bulb and keep the tips slightly above ground. Clusters of bulbs will form over the summer.

Golden Focaccia with Savory Onion Confit

On its own, rosemary focaccia can make a fun family meal—kids love to pat out the dough. Toppings to consider would be caramelized onions, pitted black olives, or even sautéed bitter greens with a sprinkle of fresh thyme. When company comes over, you can jazz the focaccia up by spreading it with this savory confit of golden-brown onions and chunky walnuts. The confit can also be used as a pasta sauce, tossed with fettuccine and Parmesan cheese.   *Serves 6*

CONFIT

2 tablespoons unsalted butter

1 tablespoon extra virgin olive oil

2 large Walla Walla onions, thinly sliced into half-moons

2 teaspoons finely chopped fresh rosemary

½ cup dry white wine

1 clove garlic, minced

¼ cup walnuts, toasted and coarsely chopped

Salt and freshly ground pepper, to taste

FOCACCIA

1 (½-ounce) package (2¼ teaspoons) active dry yeast

½ teaspoon sugar

¾ cup warm (105°F–115°F) water

¼ cup olive oil, plus more as desired

1 teaspoon sea salt

2 cups unbleached all-purpose flour, or more as needed

1 tablespoon finely chopped fresh rosemary

1 tablespoon freshly grated Parmesan cheese

1 Make the confit: In a large saucepan, heat the butter and oil over medium heat. Add the onions and 1 teaspoon of the rosemary. Cook, stirring often, until the onions are softened, about 5 minutes. Reduce the heat to low. Cook, stirring often (especially toward the end of cooking to avoid sticking), until the onions are very tender and golden brown, about 45 minutes. Stir in the wine and garlic. Bring to a boil. Reduce the heat to medium and cook until the wine has completely evaporated, about 5 minutes. Stir in the remaining teaspoon of rosemary and the walnuts. Season with salt and pepper. Cool to room temperature.

2 Make the focaccia: In a large bowl, sprinkle the yeast and sugar into the water. Let stand until the mixture looks foamy, about 10 minutes. Stir to dissolve the yeast, adding 2 tablespoons of the olive oil. Gradually stir in the salt and flour to make a stiff dough. Turn out onto a lightly floured work surface, kneading the dough with more flour as needed until the dough is smooth and elastic, about 8 minutes.

3 Lightly oil a large bowl. Place the dough in the bowl and turn to coat both sides with oil. Cover the bowl with a damp kitchen towel, and let stand in a warm place until the dough doubles in volume, about 1 hour.

4 Lightly oil a baking sheet or a 9-by-12-inch ovenproof pan. Punch down the dough and turn it out onto a lightly floured work surface. Punch and pat the dough to form a 9-by-12-inch rectangle, and transfer to the baking sheet or pan. Cover the dough with a damp kitchen towel, and let stand in a warm place until it looks puffy, about 30 minutes.

5 Meanwhile, position a rack in the center of the oven and preheat to 400°F.

6 Just before baking, poke indentations all over the dough with your fingers. Drizzle the remaining 2 tablespoons olive oil (or a bit more, to taste) on top. Sprinkle with the rosemary and Parmesan. Bake until the focaccia is golden brown on the bottom (lift up a corner to check), about 20 minutes. Remove from the oven and cool on the sheet for a few minutes, then spread with the confit and cut into generous squares.

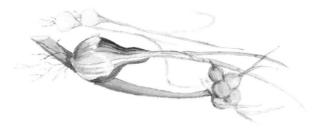

Butternut Squash Bisque

Of the many varieties of winter squash, butternut is my favorite for soup because of its smooth texture, bright color, and mellow flavor. Unlike other soups, this bisque can be ready to serve piping hot at the table in less than an hour. *Serves 4 to 6*

2 tablespoons olive oil

2 tablespoons unsalted butter

1 large onion, peeled and coarsely chopped

1 clove garlic

Salt and freshly ground pepper, to taste

1 teaspoon curry powder

½ teaspoon ground ginger

¼ teaspoon coriander

⅛ teaspoon cumin

¼ teaspoon turmeric

1 butternut squash

2 tablespoons cider syrup (concentrated cider) or pure maple syrup

4 cups chicken broth

Crème fraîche, for garnish

1 In a large stockpot, heat the olive oil and butter over medium heat. Add the onion and garlic, season with salt and pepper, and sauté, stirring frequently, until softened, 5–10 minutes. Add the curry, ginger, coriander, cumin, and turmeric. Continue to stir until the flavors have blended, about 10 minutes total.

2 Peel the squash, using a vegetable peeler. Slice the squash in half lengthwise, then cut into quarters. Remove the seeds, cube into 1-inch chunks, and add to the sautéed onions. Douse with the cider or maple syrup and cook for 3–5 minutes, stirring to blend flavors.

3 Add the chicken broth and stir to combine. Turn the heat to medium-low, and allow the soup to simmer for 30 minutes, or until the squash is softened.

4 With an immersion blender, purée the soup. Serve with a dollop of crème fraîche.

Arugula Salad with Lemon Vinaigrette

For a refreshing splash of summer, use this lemony vinaigrette dressing on a variety of spring greens; it is especially good for bringing out the tart notes in arugula. This dish is easy to make ahead and ideal for potluck; add the arugula greens just before serving. *Serves 4 to 6*

1 cup vegetable stock or water

1 cup whole-wheat couscous

1 cup dry green or black lentils

¼ cup Lemon Vinaigrette (see below), or more, to taste

4 cups fresh arugula, washed and dried

6 scallions or 1 small yellow onion, coarsely chopped

1 cup cherry tomatoes, halved

1 cucumber, peeled, seeded, and diced into ½-inch cubes

½ cup feta cheese, crumbled

1 In a medium saucepan, bring the stock or water to a boil. Add the couscous, cover, turn off the heat, and allow to sit until all the liquid has been absorbed, about 10 minutes.

2 In a separate saucepan, cover the lentils with enough water to cover them by 1 inch, and simmer over medium heat until tender, about 15 minutes. Be careful not to overcook, or the lentils will fall apart in the salad. Drain any excess water and cool.

3 In a large salad bowl, combine the lentils and couscous and toss with half the lemon vinaigrette. Just before serving, coarsely chop the arugula and combine it with the lentils and couscous, along with the scallions, cherry tomatoes, and cucumbers. Crumble on the feta cheese, and add more dressing, to taste.

Lemon Vinaigrette *Makes ½ cup*

½ cup extra virgin olive oil

¼ cup fresh lemon juice (about 2 lemons)

¼ cup red wine vinegar

1 tablespoon Dijon mustard

2 cloves garlic, mashed

Salt and freshly ground pepper, to taste

Combine all the ingredients in a Mason jar with a lid. Shake to blend until emulsified. Set aside until the salad is prepared.

Leg of Lamb Infused with Rosemary and Ginger

Lamb is a special-occasion food, which makes it the perfect choice for a festive family dinner. The key is to carve small pockets in it to insert the herbs and garlic, then allow the marinade to smother the leg of lamb for at least 12 hours before cooking.   *Serves 8*

MARINADE (makes 1 cup)

6 cloves garlic, peeled

¼ cup coarsely chopped crystallized ginger

¼ cup Dijon mustard

¼ cup balsamic vinegar

½ cup olive oil

2 heaping tablespoons fresh rosemary, removed from stem

2 heaping tablespoons fresh thyme, removed from stem

3 tablespoons tamari or soy sauce

LAMB

1 (8-pound) leg of lamb

1 Prepare the marinade: In a food processor fitted with a steel blade, blend all the ingredients until a smooth paste forms.

2 Trim excess fat from the lamb. With a sharp knife, cut 1-inch slits all over. Using a small spoon, insert garlic-herb paste into each slit, reserving a small amount. Rub the remaining paste over the lamb. Place in a roasting pan large enough to hold the lamb, cover tightly with plastic wrap, and refrigerate overnight or up to 24 hours.

3 Preheat the oven to 325°F. Remove the plastic wrap and cook the lamb for about 1½ hours. (Allow 18 minutes per pound for well-done meat, 15 minutes for medium-rare, and 12 minutes for rare.) The lamb will continue to cook after it is removed from the oven, so do not overcook. Transfer the lamb to a carving board and loosely cover with foil or a tea towel to keep warm. Allow the roast to sit for 30 minutes before carving it into thin slices.

Caramelized Shallot Custard

Deeply colored and intensely flavored, caramelized shallots give these individual custards the look and texture of a pâté and an almost indefinable taste. *Serves 8*

1 tablespoon olive oil

12 shallots (about 1 pound), peeled but kept whole

1 cup vegetable broth or water

1 teaspoon finely chopped fresh sage

1 tablespoon sugar

1½ tablespoons dry sherry

1½ cups heavy cream

4 large eggs

4 large egg yolks

½ teaspoon salt

⅛ teaspoon freshly ground pepper

Small sage leaves, for garnish

1 Heat the oil in a medium skillet over low heat. Add the shallots and cook, stirring often, until golden brown on all sides, about 30 minutes. Add the broth and sage and increase the heat to medium. Cook at a rapid simmer, stirring occasionally, until the liquid has evaporated and the shallots are tender, about 10 minutes.

2 Sprinkle with the sugar and cook, occasionally shaking the pan, until the shallots are glazed, about 1 minute. Sprinkle with the sherry. Scrape the shallots and their juices into a food processor or blender and purée. You should have about ½ cup shallot purée.

3 Position a rack in the center of the oven and preheat to 350°F. Lightly butter eight 4-ounce ramekins.

4 Whip together the cream, eggs, yolks, shallot purée, salt, and pepper until well combined. Pour equal quantities into the ramekins. Place the ramekins in a large roasting pan, and pour enough hot water into the pan to come halfway up the sides of the ramekins. Cover the entire pan loosely with aluminum foil.

5 Bake until the custards are set when given a shake, about 20 minutes. Let stand for 5 minutes. Run a knife around the inside of each, and invert to unmold. Garnish with a small sage leaf and serve hot.

Vermont Carrot Cake with Maple Frosting

When it's time to bake a layer cake for a celebration, this maple-flavored carrot cake can't be beat. I keep a gallon of dark, Grade B maple syrup for cooking and baking, and reserve the milder Grade A syrup to pour onto pancakes. *Makes one 9-inch round layer cake*

CAKE

2 cups unbleached all-purpose flour,

2 teaspoons baking powder

2 teaspoons baking soda

½ teaspoon ground cinnamon

¼ teaspoon ground ginger

⅛ teaspoon grated nutmeg

1 teaspoon salt

1 teaspoon pure vanilla extract

1 cup pure maple syrup, preferably Grade B

1 cup granulated sugar

½ cup vegetable oil

4 large eggs, at room temperature

3 cups shredded carrots (about 1 pound), plus ½ cup

FROSTING

1 cup confectioner's sugar

1 (8-ounce) package cream cheese, at room temperature

4 tablespoons (½ stick) unsalted butter, at room temperature

1 teaspoon pure vanilla extract

¼ cup pure maple syrup, preferably Grade B

1 Position a rack in the center of the oven and preheat to 350°F. Butter and lightly flour two 9-inch round cake pans.

2 To make the cake: Sift the flour, baking powder, baking soda, cinnamon, ginger, nutmeg, and salt into a medium bowl. In another medium bowl, whisk together the vanilla, maple syrup, sugar, and oil, then whisk in the eggs, one at a time. Gradually stir in the flour mixture, and then add 3 cups carrots. Stir to combine, and pour the batter evenly into the prepared pans.

3 Bake until the cakes spring back when pressed in the center, about 45 minutes. Cool on a wire rack for 10 minutes. Run a knife around the insides of the pans, and invert the cakes onto the rack. Turn right side up and cool completely.

4 To make the frosting: In a food processor, pulse the confectioner's sugar, cream cheese, butter, and vanilla to blend. With the motor running, gradually add enough maple syrup to make a smooth frosting, stopping the motor and scraping down the sides of the bowl.

5 Place one cake layer, rounded side down, on a serving plate. Spread ½ cup of the frosting on the layer. Top with the second layer, rounded side up. Spread the top and then the sides with the remaining frosting. Spread and gently press the remaining ½ cup grated carrots on top.

Fresh Strawberry Crème Tart

This old-fashioned dessert in a sweet tart shell is still my favorite way to celebrate the arrival of the strawberry season. Select the freshest, most beautiful berries.   *Serves 8*

4 cups whole strawberries, washed, stem ends removed

¾ cup plus 1 tablespoon sugar, divided

1½ cups plus 1 tablespoon unbleached white flour, divided

½ teaspoon salt

9 tablespoons (1 stick plus 1 tablespoon) cold unsalted butter, cut into small pieces

½ cup water chilled with ice cubes

¾ cup milk

½ vanilla bean, split lengthwise

3 egg yolks

Lemon verbena, finely chopped, for garnish

1 Place the strawberries in a bowl, sprinkle with ½ cup of the sugar, and set aside to macerate for 30 minutes at room temperature.

2 Sift the 1½ cups flour, salt, and 1 tablespoon sugar into a bowl. With your fingers, rub the butter into the flour mixture until it resembles coarse crumbs. Sprinkle with 3 tablespoons of the ice water. Work the dough on a floured surface until it just holds together, adding more ice water as needed. Wrap the dough and refrigerate for 30 minutes or longer.

3 Place the milk and vanilla bean in a heavy saucepan. Bring almost to a boil over medium heat, then remove the pan from the heat and cool. Remove the vanilla bean.

4 In a separate bowl, whisk the egg yolks and the remaining ¼ cup sugar until blended. Sprinkle in the 1 tablespoon flour, then gradually whisk in the heated milk. Return the mixture to the saucepan, and cook over medium heat, stirring, until thickened and custardlike, about 10 minutes.

5 Set up a strainer over a bowl or a large measuring cup with a spout, and pour the custard through, pushing with a wooden spoon. Set aside to cool completely.

6 Preheat the oven to 400°F. Bring the dough out of the refrigerator and roll it out on a floured surface to as thin as you can, about ¼ inch. Fold it in half, transfer it to a 9-inch tart pan, and trim to fit. Crimp the edges, and prick the dough all over with a fork.

7 Cover the dough with foil and fill with dried beans. Bake for 15 minutes. Remove the foil and beans, then continue baking until the shell is golden, 10–15 minutes. Remove from the oven and cool.

8 Stir the macerated juice from the strawberries into the pastry cream and incorporate completely. Spread the cream evenly over the baked tart shell. Arrange the strawberries upright, cut edge facing down, on the custard. Garnish with the lemon verbena and serve.

The Artist's Garden
Colorful Parterres

Garden Personality: *This garden is all about the visual qualities of vegetables. You can build an exotic tapestry of color using seeds and plants as your paintbrush and the freshly tilled soil as your blank canvas. Combine the ferny texture of carrot tops with the undulating leaves of arugula and the crimson red of radicchio, and you have a fun, colorful, and whimsical garden, framed by geometric raised beds.*

Plan to build this garden with raised beds, and add a focal point such as a simple bamboo pole structure surrounded by fragrant lemon thyme and lemon gem marigolds. Loose-leaf lettuce, Italian chicories, and bok choy cabbage are valued as tender salad greens, yet also form an eye-pleasing carpet of green, so harvest carefully to keep them growing strong.

"I like to plant close so that the leaves blend together seamlessly," says Ilona Bell, a professor at Williams College and an avid gardener. She designs her kitchen garden with an artist's eye and has an unusual knack for combining edible plants that weave together as if they were inseparable friends. Her Artist's Garden is remarkably productive, though I suspect the plants are selected as much for their brilliant colors as for the flavors they provide in the kitchen. Entering under a tall trellis smothered in a canary-yellow clematis vine, you are reminded that the vegetable world is rich in color and texture. You are greeted by ferny carrots, Troutback lettuce, and garlic scapes accentuated by a handmade trellis for painted runner beans, a twig bench beneath an arbor, and rustic sticks that stake the eggplant. It's these visual flourishes that distinguish Ilona's garden and give it personality.

Ten Tips for Growing an Artist's Garden

1 Keep a garden notebook of great combinations or changes for the following year.

2 Sowing seeds directly in the garden rather than starting with plants will provide a longer season of greenery.

3 Form paths with bluestone pavers or another flat stone that will provide sure footing and keep borders neat.

4 Enrich the soil every year by planting fall cover crops and using aged compost.

5 Hand-dig each bed with a garden fork rather than using a rototiller, in order to keep the lower layers of the soil and natural microorganisms healthy.

6 Build a variety of trellises to allow plants to grow at different heights.

7 Consider a nook area for a garden bench. This is an ideal place for sketching or taking garden notes.

8 Asparagus and other perennial garden plants, such as blueberries or espaliered apple trees, will provide long-term ornamental edibles.

9 Install a good fence with wire mesh along the interior to keep out rabbits and other diggers.

10 Encourage whimsy; collect garden ornaments that enhance your pleasure and bring a smile.

OVERALL SIZE: *40 feet by 40 feet*
BED SIZE: *(4) 10-foot by 10-foot L-shaped beds*
(4) inner triangles
(2) outer long beds
PATH WIDTH: *3 feet / 1 foot between triangles and beds / 2 feet from fence*
BEDS: *Raised beds / cypress*
PATH MATERIAL: *Bluestone stepping-stones*

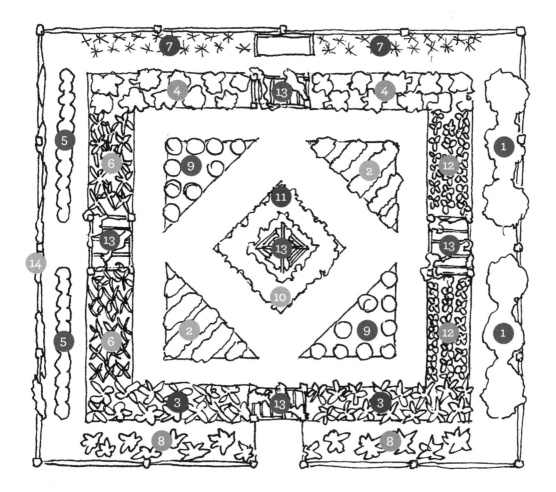

The Artist's Garden Plant List

1 Asparagus

2 Basil: Fino Verde and Red Rubin

3 Beets: Chioggia

4 Bush Beans: Royal Burgundy

5 Cabbage: Red Pac Choi

6 Carrots: Mokum

7 Garlic: Spanish Roja

8 Golden Tomatillos (Husk Cherries): Pineapple

9 Lettuce: Mixed Head

10 Marigolds: Lemon Gem

11 Nasturtiums: Moonlight and Empress of India

12 Onions: Red Torpedo

13 Pole Beans: Indian Runner

14 Sunflowers: Zebulon and Chocolate

① Asparagus

Asparagus produces young edible shoots in the spring, and is one of the best-known and widely planted herbaceous perennial plants. Asparagus will be in the ground for a long time, so it makes sense to take the time to build proper soil in advance. Asparagus does not tolerate saturated soil conditions, so choose a well-drained location in full sun. Plant crowns in a trench, fill with compost and a handful of high-phosphate organic fertilizer to give the roots a boost, but hold back on the nitrogen and the potassium. Once planted, it's best to leave asparagus for several seasons before harvesting the first spears.

③ Beets and Beet Greens

Beets are grown primarily for their roots, but you can also choose a variety that is prized for its leaves as well as its underground bulb. These will grow all summer, adding color to your salads, if you keep the tops trimmed. Harvest frequently to keep the greens growing, as the beet roots will develop over time. Direct sow seeds in the garden in prepared loose soil. Seeds can be planted in a row; allow ½ inch between seeds and 5 inches between rows in order to cultivate. Keep plants watered and harvest with scissors when 5 to 8 inches tall. Favorites for green tops: Bull's Blood, Perpetual Spinach. Favorites for roots: Chioggia, Golden Beet, Merlin, and Forono.

Cabbage

Homegrown cabbage is a prized ornamental edible. Plan to alternate green, red, and savory-leaved varieties for a full spectrum of plants that will continue to grow late into the fall. Sow seeds in pots in late May, or purchase plants and transplant into the garden. Allow plenty of space to grow. Favorites: Tendersweet, Caraflex, Farao, Vertus Savoy, Bok Choy.

Garlic

Garlic is a crop that is both ornamental and essential for a kitchen garden. It is best when planted in the fall and harvested the following summer. Seed and plant catalogs offer a variety of soft-neck and hard-neck varieties, from Italian red-skinned to huge but mild elephant garlic. All are good, so try a variety, and when you find one you like, save a few to replant the following year. Break apart a head of garlic, and plant individual cloves.

###

Tomatillos

The secret to every good salsa, tomatillos are easy to grow and remarkably productive. Plant them along with tomatoes, and plan to harvest the pods when the fruit appears from the papery husks. Cape Gooseberries, also in the Physalis family, tend to grow low to the ground, and the fruits are small and sweet, typically eaten as a cherry tomato. Plant in pots and transplant into the garden. Favorites: Pineapple, Purple, Toma Verde, Verde Puebla.

Asparagus Soup with Coconut Lemon Crème

The first tender spears of asparagus are best enjoyed fresh and whole from the garden, but as the season progresses, the stalks get larger, and the crop more abundant, this is an excellent soup to prepare. Its light, lemony flavors blended with a hint of curry are delicious served warm or chilled, and topped with crème fraîche. *Serves 4 to 6*

2 tablespoons unsalted butter

2 tablespoons olive oil

1 medium onion, finely chopped

Dash salt

½ teaspoon curry powder

¼ teaspoon ground ginger

Zest and juice of 1 lemon

4 medium red-skinned potatoes, peeled and cut into ½-inch dice (2 cups)

3 cups vegetable or chicken broth

1 cup (8-ounce can) coconut milk

12 to 18 asparagus spears, trimmed and cut into ½-inch lengths (2 cups)

GARNISH

1 cup crème fraîche

Scallions or chives, finely chopped, to taste

Salt and freshly ground pepper, to taste

1 In a large pot over medium heat, melt the butter and oil. Add the onion and salt and sauté, stirring often, until the onion is golden, about 5 minutes.

2 Stir in the curry powder, ginger, and half of the lemon zest and juice. Then add the potatoes and simmer, stirring occasionally, to blend the flavors, about 5 minutes.

3 Slowly add the broth, coconut milk, and asparagus and bring to a simmer over medium heat. Cover partially and continue to cook until the potatoes are tender, about 20 minutes.

4 With an immersion blender, or in a food processor, purée the mixture until smooth. In a small bowl, blend the crème fraîche, remaining lemon zest and juice, scallions or chives, and salt and pepper.

5 Serve the soup warm, garnished with a swirl of the seasoned crème fraîche.

Basil Pesto Swirl Bread

Looking for a surefire hit to bring to a potluck? Try this crusty French loaf with a swirl of savory pesto, rolled and sliced into individual rolls. To save time, prepare the pesto while the bread is rising.   *Makes 24 rolls*

¼-ounce package (2½ teaspoons) active dry yeast

1 teaspoon sugar

1½ cup warm (105°F–115°F) water

4 tablespoons (½ stick) unsalted butter, melted and cooled to lukewarm

1 teaspoon sea salt

5 cups unbleached all-purpose flour, as needed

Oil for baking pan

1 cup Basil Pesto (see page 102)

1 Sprinkle the yeast and sugar over the water in a large bowl. Let stand until the mixture looks foamy, about 10 minutes. Stir in the butter and salt. Gradually stir in enough of the flour to make a stiff dough. Turn out onto a lightly floured work surface and knead, adding more flour as required, until the dough is smooth and elastic, about 10 minutes. Gather the dough into a ball.

2 Lightly oil a large bowl. Place the dough in the bowl and turn to coat the dough with the oil. Cover the bowl with a damp kitchen towel, and let stand in a warm place until the dough has doubled in volume, about 1 hour. Punch down the dough, turn out onto a lightly floured work surface, and knead briefly.

3 Divide the dough in half. Working with one section at a time, roll the dough into a rectangle 12 inches long and 8 inches wide.

Spread the dough with the pesto, leaving a ½-inch border on all sides. Starting at the long end, roll up into a tight cylinder, pinch the seams closed, and pinch the long end closed.

4 Using a sharp knife, cut the loaves into 1-inch-thick rounds. Lightly oil two 12-cup muffin tins, and place 1 round of dough in each of the 24 cups. Cover the tins with a damp kitchen towel and let them stand in a warm place until the rolls look puffy, about 30 minutes.

5 Preheat the oven to 375°F. Place a rack in the center of the oven, and bake the rolls until golden brown, about 20 minutes. Remove from the oven and allow the rolls to cool for a few minutes before popping them out of the pan.

Bean and Potato Salad with Warm Mustard Vinaigrette

Fingerling potatoes, with their light, creamy texture, are a highly prized culinary treasure. Growing no bigger than an average finger (hence their name), they are the perfect salad potato. They can be found at farmers' markets but are easy to grow in your own kitchen garden. Added while warm, the herbed vinaigrette penetrates and marinates, bringing all the flavors together. *Serves 4 to 6*

6 slices bacon

2 shallots, finely chopped

¼ cup red wine vinegar

1 teaspoon Dijon mustard

1 teaspoon whole-grain mustard, such as Moutarde de Meaux

½ cup extra virgin olive oil

2 pounds (about 8) fingerling potatoes, scrubbed and peeled

½ pound purple or green snap beans (about 2 cups)

2 medium red bell peppers, roasted and cut into ¼-inch wedges

4 red scallions, finely chopped

Coarse sea salt and freshly ground pepper, to taste

¼ cup finely minced fresh mixed herbs (summer savory, chives, parsley, sweet basil)

1 Cook the bacon in a skillet over medium heat until crisp and brown, about 8 minutes. Using a slotted spatula, transfer to paper towels to drain and cool, and set aside.

2 Drain excess bacon grease from the pan, reserving a thin layer (2 tablespoons) in the skillet. Heat over low to medium heat, add the shallots, and simmer until golden brown, about 3 minutes. Gradually pour in the vinegar, the mustards, and then the oil, and stir with a wooden spoon to deglaze the pan. Whisk to emulsify the dressing and set aside.

3 Drop the potatoes into salted boiling water, and cook until tender but not falling apart, 15–20 minutes. Drain in a colander to re-lease excess moisture. Cut the potatoes into ¼-inch-thick rounds and place in a wooden salad bowl. Toss with the dressing and leave at room temperature.

4 Drop the beans into salted boiling water, and cook for 3–5 minutes, until you hear them snap (hence the name "snap bean"); this indicates they are tender. Drain and rinse under cold water, and pat dry. Cut the beans on the diagonal into 1-inch lengths and toss into the salad bowl, together with the potatoes, red pepper wedges, and scallions.

5 Coat with the dressing, then crumble the bacon on top, and season with salt, pepper, and the herbs.

Strip Steak with Garlic Scapes

In the spring, garlic planted the previous fall will send up seedpods, called scapes, which should be removed in order to let the garlic underground continue to grow. Trim these off, chop them, and use them in place of garlic in various dishes, including this simple presentation of strip steaks. Naturally, be sure to buy meat that is locally grown and pasture fed for the best flavor and value.   *Serves 4*

2 tablespoons olive oil

2 tablespoons unsalted butter, divided

4 (6-ounce) strip steaks

½ teaspoon coarse sea salt

¼ teaspoon freshly ground pepper

½ cup finely chopped garlic scapes

½ cup superior-quality balsamic vinegar

1 Heat the olive oil and 1 tablespoon of the butter in a cast-iron or heavy-bottomed skillet over medium-high heat.

2 Season the steaks with the salt and pepper and add them to the hot pan. Sear for 4 minutes on one side, flip and cook another 2 minutes, and push the steaks aside in the pan, while still cooking.

3 Melt the remaining 1 tablespoon butter in the pan next to the steaks and add the garlic scapes. Sauté, stirring frequently, for 2 minutes, until softened. Add the vinegar to deglaze the pan, stirring and scraping all the flavorful bits and pieces. Spoon the scapes and vinegar over the steaks in the pan and continue to cook for another few minutes, until the sauce is slightly thickened and glazed.

4 Transfer the steaks to serving plates. Spoon the seasoned scapes over the steaks, pouring the rest of the sauce over them before serving.

Beets and Greens with Aioli

Aioli is simply homemade mayonnaise with a strong garlic accent. It brings out the flavor of vegetables like no other sauce, and the mellow yellow color is especially stunning against the deep green and red of the beets. Seek out young, tender beets, and select only the best beet greens for this delectable side dish. *Serves 4*

6– 8 smallish beets, with greens attached

2 tablespoons extra virgin olive oil

Salt and freshly ground pepper

Aioli (see below)

1 Preheat the oven to 350°F.

2 Rinse the beets and greens to remove all soil. Cut the greens from the beets, leaving 2-inch stalks. Set the beet tops aside.

3 Place the beets in a baking dish, drizzle with the olive oil, and cover loosely with foil. Bake until the beets are soft, about 45 minutes. Pierce through with a sharp knife to check for doneness. Remove from the oven; cool, peel, and chop into quarters or ½-inch cubes.

4 Coarsely chop the greens into 2-inch sections, and measure out about 8 cups. Drop into a kettle of boiling salted water, and cook for 5 minutes, or until wilted. Drain and run under cool water. Gently squeeze out the excess liquid.

5 Divide the greens evenly onto four small plates. Drizzle the greens with 1 tablespoon aioli and top with quartered beets. Add more aioli if desired, and season with salt and pepper to taste.

Aioli *Makes ½ cup*

4 medium garlic cloves

¼ teaspoon salt

2 egg yolks

½ cup olive oil

2 teaspoons lemon juice (½ lemon) or tarragon vinegar

⅛ teaspoon freshly ground pepper

1 Press the garlic cloves through a garlic press into a medium bowl. Add the salt, then the egg yolks, one at a time, beating a whisk until combined.

2 Slowly drip in the oil, beating constantly. When the sauce begins to thicken, stir in the lemon juice or tarragon vinegar, then continue to add the oil, beating vigorously until the sauce becomes thickened. Add ground pepper, stir well, and refrigerate.

Cape Gooseberry Clafoutis

Cape gooseberries, or husk cherries, are in the tomatillo family, yet are sweet and small like currant cherry tomatoes. Each plant is prolific, and there are plenty for fresh eating as well as for this satisfying clafoutis, which is a thick crepe batter baked in the oven. Serve for dessert or as a special breakfast treat. *Makes one 9-inch tart*

1 tablespoon unsalted butter, to grease skillet

1 tablespoon vanilla extract

6 eggs

6 tablespoons sugar

1¼ cups milk

2 tablespoons kirsch

Pinch salt

¾ cup flour

3 cups cape gooseberries (or husk cherries), peeled from husks and cut in half

Confectioner's sugar, for dusting

1 Preheat the oven to 425°F. Generously butter a 9-inch cast-iron skillet or baking dish.

2 In a blender, combine the vanilla extract, eggs, sugar, milk, kirsch, and salt. Blend for a few seconds to mix the ingredients, then add the flour and blend until smooth, about 1 minute.

3 Pour the batter into the skillet or baking dish, then distribute the gooseberries evenly over the top. Bake until a skewer inserted into the center comes out clean and a golden crust has formed on the top and bottom of the clafoutis, about 30 minutes. Dust with confectioner's sugar.

The Country Garden
Easy Maintenance

Garden Personality: This is a workhorse of a garden, ideal for the gardener who likes to pack a lot into a small space. The Country Garden is designed with intensive garden beds that are mounded to accommodate thick rows of plants. Be prepared with plenty of recipes when the harvest season kicks in.

The Country Garden contains all the familiar elements of a classic kitchen garden, but with extra wide paths for a wheelbarrow, a central axis with evenly spaced beds, and an ample border for cutting flowers such as zinnias, dahlias, and sunflowers. A clearly defined entrance forms a transition from the lawn into the garden, with a two-bin compost pile and a generous tool shed easily accessible. Permaculture is a way of working the landscape naturally, and this garden design blends some of the key elements to avoid disrupting the natural balance, while increasing productivity in the food garden.

If the area you've chosen is especially wild and weedy, it's best to start building this Country Garden in the fall, to allow ample time to prepare the beds and fully remove the weeds. Stretch a layer of black plastic or cardboard weighted down with bales of hay over the entire garden area for the winter, to completely choke out weeds. In the spring, remove the layers and measure and map out the garden beds. Once the beds are in place, and you are ready to plant, you can mulch the paths to keep weeds from resprouting by spreading a layer of wet newspaper and then piling on several inches of straw, hay, or cedar bark.

Intermingling plants that complement each other is called companion planting, and it creates a naturally symbiotic relationship between groupings. Tall plants will tower in the center, with midsize plants on the edges, and the smaller plants tucked underneath. Classic pairings are tomatoes with marigolds, cucumbers with dill, beans with carrots, beets with onions, and chervil with lettuce. The result is a super productive kitchen garden, grown in a small space.

Ten Tips for Growing a Country Garden

1 For long-term benefit, take extra care to prepare the soil and remove all weeds and grass before planting. It is ideal to start preparing in the fall for a spring planting.

2 For optimal performance and longevity, plan to grow half the plants from transplants, and the other half using direct-sown seeds.

3 Make a list of companion-plant combinations and place them together in the garden beds.

4 Be aware of the heights for each plant, and place taller plants in the center, medium size in the center, and the shorter plants along the edges.

5 Think vertical; grow cucumbers and other vines upward on a trellis to save space.

6 Observe how the sun hits the garden, and plant tall plants such as sunflowers or peas in the back rows, to keep a full sun exposure to all the plants.

7 Enclose the garden with a picket fence encased with chicken wire, to prevent small animals from entering.

8 Site the garden near a hose for irrigation and rinsing vegetables.

9 Mulch the paths with a thick bed of straw or hay.

10 Build an arbor to connect the garden with the tool shed and to create a bit of shade for the gardener.

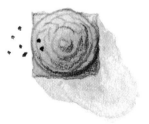

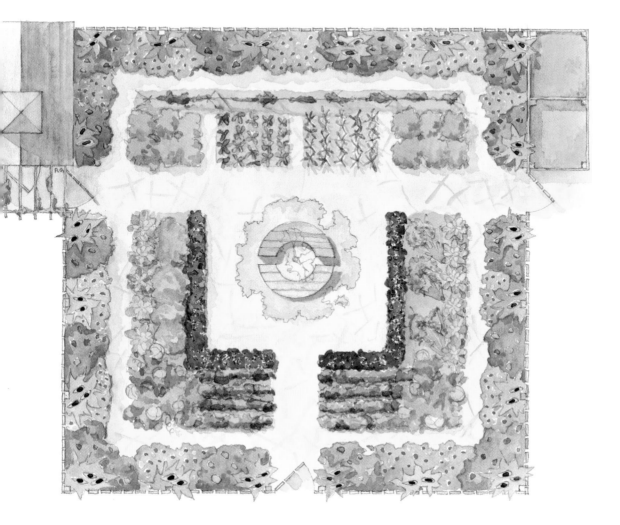

OVERALL SIZE: *26 feet by 28 feet*
BED SIZE: *4 feet*
CENTRAL BED: *5 feet*
PATH WIDTH: *3 feet*

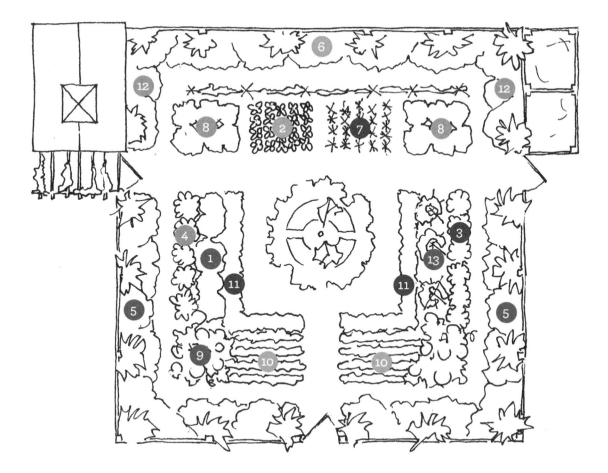

Country Garden Plant List

1. Beans: Dragon Tongue
2. Beets: Chioggia and Golden
3. Cauliflower: Graffiti Purple
4. Collards: Flash
5. Flowers (Mixed Border): Sunflowers, Dahlias, and Zinnia
6. Herbs: Sweet Genovese Basil, Italian Flat-Leaf Parsley, and Chervil
7. Leeks: King Richard (early) and Tadorna (late)
8. Lettuce: Mixed Butterhead
9. Melons: Charantais
10. Potatoes: Purple Peruvian and Yukon Gold
11. Radishes: d'Avignon
12. Rhubarb
13. Tomatoes: Yellow and Red Pear, Cherokee Purple, and Green Zebra

2 Beets

Beets are grown primarily for their roots, but you can also choose a variety that is prized for its leaves as well as its underground bulb. Harvest frequently to keep the greens growing, as the beet roots will develop over time. Direct sow seeds in the garden in prepared loose soil. Seeds can be planted in a row; allow ½ inch between seeds and 5 inches between rows in order to cultivate. Keep plants watered and harvest with scissors when 5 to 8 inches tall. Favorites for green tops: Bull's Blood, Perpetual Spinach. Favorites for roots: Chioggia, Golden Beet, Merlin, Forono.

9 Melons

While Vermont summers are not ideal for growing melons, I am hooked on the depth of flavor that a vine-ripened fruit offers compared to the commercially produced grocery-store fruit, which is picked while still green in anticipation of ripening. Most people know how to smell the stem end to tell when it is ripe, but true vine-ripened fruit slips right off the stem. Reserving a small corner of the garden for melons is worthwhile, especially if you live in a temperate climate. Prestart seeds in small individual pots four to six weeks before the frost-free date and transplant into hills of three plants each when temperatures are steadily above freezing. Keep plants watered, and trim off branches that do not contain flowers, to concentrate the plant's energy on ripening the fruit. Favorites: Charentais, Galia, Ogen, Blenheim Orange, Moon and Stars.

11 Radishes

Radishes are a familiar garden crop, ideal for a Children's Garden, since they grow quickly and are easy to pluck out of the ground. However, few children—or adults—actually relish the flavor of radishes, and they are most frequently used as a garnish. Seeds are direct sown in a row, and can be blended with carrots in the same row, allowing the radishes to push up first, and naturally thinning out the row of carrots that will follow. Favorites: d'Avignon, Easter Egg, Reisenrot.

12 Rhubarb

A true harbinger of spring, a single rhubarb plant will easily yield enough for a family of four. It is also a highly ornamental plant in the kitchen garden. A single leaf will grow to a foot in diameter, and the plant can grow to several feet tall, so be sure to allow plenty of room. It's best to purchase rhubarb crowns, rather than start from seeds, and plant them in the early spring or late fall. A cool-season perennial, rhubarb requires temperatures below 40°F to break dormancy and stimulate spring growth, as well as summer temperatures averaging 75°F. Plant in full sun or partial shade, bury the rhizome to the level of the crown, and keep the plants watered until established (as well as during dry weather). Harvest by gently yanking at the base of a stalk, and remove the stem.

Caramelized Onion Tart

For this recipe, you will need a well-flavored yellow onion that is neither too sharp nor too sweet—try the lovely Giallo di Milano, a superior Italian variety. Slow cooking brings out every drop of sweetness in an onion, which is balanced here by the sherry or balsamic vinegar.

Makes one 10-inch square tart

PASTRY

1½ cups unbleached all-purpose flour

1 teaspoon dried rosemary

½ teaspoon dried thyme

½ teaspoon salt

8 tablespoons (1 stick) chilled unsalted
butter, cut into ½-inch pieces

½ cup yogurt

FILLING

2 tablespoons olive oil

2 tablespoons unsalted butter

3 large sweet onions, thinly sliced

2 teaspoons light brown sugar

½ teaspoon sea salt

⅛ teaspoon freshly ground pepper

¼ cup Marsala sherry or balsamic vinegar

1 large egg

2 cups ricotta cheese

1 teaspoon finely chopped fresh thyme

1 tablespoon chopped fresh rosemary

½ cup shredded sharp cheddar cheese

¼ cup finely grated Parmesan cheese
(grated with a microplane zester)

1 Make the pastry: In the bowl of a food processor fitted with a steel blade, blend together the flour, rosemary, thyme, and salt, and work until mixed. With the motor on, add the butter, one piece at a time. Add the yogurt and blend until the dough forms a ball, less than 1 minute. Roll the dough out onto a lightly floured work surface, into an 11- to 12-inch-wide circle about ⅛ inch thick. Transfer the dough to a 9-inch pie plate, trimming the overhang to ½ inch around the sides. Fold the edges under and crimp the edge of the dough. Refrigerate.

2 Meanwhile, make the filling: In a large skillet, melt the oil and butter over medium heat. Add the onions and cook, stirring often, until they soften. Stir in the sugar, salt, and pepper; reduce the heat to low and sauté, stirring frequently, until the onions are deeply browned and have a sticky texture, about 30 minutes. Stir in the sherry or vinegar, and gently cook for another 2 minutes. Remove from the heat and set aside.

3 Position a rack in the center of the oven and preheat to 375°F. Beat the egg in a medium bowl, then stir in the ricotta, thyme, and rosemary. Add the cheddar cheese and stir. Spread the mixture evenly in the pastry shell and distribute the caramelized onions on top. Sprinkle with the Parmesan cheese.

4 Bake until the pastry is golden brown, 35–40 minutes. Let stand for 10 minutes before cutting. Serve warm.

Roasted Beet and Walnut Salad

Chioggia, or candy-striped beets, are not only the sweetest beets around, they also look terrific in a salad. If possible, use them in this chunky dish to show them off. Beets of any color will also be delicious, but keep in mind that red beets will bleed. A tart apple is in order here—in Vermont, we would choose a McIntosh or Macoun. *Serves 4*

6 medium beets, scrubbed and trimmed

2 tart apples, peeled, cored, and cut into ½-inch cubes

½ cup walnuts, toasted

½ cup (4 ounces) crumbled feta cheese

½ cup fresh chopped Italian flat-leaf parsley

1 small red onion, thinly sliced

½ cup extra virgin olive oil

¼ cup balsamic vinegar

2 tablespoons finely chopped shallot

½ teaspoon Dijon mustard

Salt and freshly ground pepper, to taste

1 Position a rack in the center of the oven and preheat to 400°F. Wrap each beet in aluminum foil and place on a baking sheet. Bake until the beets are tender, about 1 hour. Cool completely. Peel the beets and cut into ½-inch cubes.

2 Mix the beets, apples, walnuts, feta, parsley, and onion in a salad bowl.

3 In a small saucepan, heat the olive oil; add the vinegar, shallot, and mustard, whisking often until simmering, about 5 minutes. Mix as much dressing as you like into the salad, reserving any remaining dressing for another use. Season the salad with salt and pepper. The salad can be made up to 2 hours ahead, covered and refrigerated.

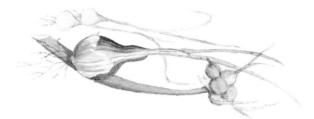

Smoked Trout with Creamy Herbed Horseradish Dressing

Smoked trout in the spring is a sure sign of good things to come. Mache with mixed greens, topped by smoked trout and a creamy horseradish dressing, creates the perfect appetizer salad or amuse-bouche. *Serves 4*

2 tablespoons Prepared Horseradish (see below)

½ cup crème fraîche

⅓ cup finely chopped mixed fresh chives, dill, and Italian flat-leaf parsley

Salt and freshly ground pepper, to taste

1 head butterhead lettuce, torn into bite-size pieces

1 cup mixed mesclun greens, washed and dried

1 cup mache, washed and dried

4 ounces smoked trout fillet

4 scallions, chopped

1 tablespoon capers (optional)

1 To make the dressing, combine the prepared horseradish, crème fraîche, chopped herbs, salt, and pepper in a glass bowl. Set aside.

2 In a wooden salad bowl, lightly toss together the lettuce, mesclun, and mache. Evenly arrange the greens on four chilled salad plates.

3 With your fingers or a knife, coarsely crumble the smoked trout over the greens, and drizzle 2 tablespoons of the dressing over each plate. Top with the scallions and capers, if using, and serve. (Reserve any leftover dressing in the refrigerator for up to 1 week.)

Prepared Horseradish

Protect your eyes, because this horseradish takes over the kitchen. *Makes 2 half-pint jars*

1 cup grated fresh horseradish root

½ cup white vinegar

¼ teaspoon salt

Combine grated horseradish root with the vinegar and salt. Pack into 2 clean half-pint jars and seal. Keep refrigerated.

Melon Mousse and Strawberry Parfait

The orange-fleshed Charentais melon—a type of cantaloupe with smooth skin, intoxicating aroma, and superior flavor—is my first choice for this silky-smooth dessert. Use the very best and ripest cantaloupe you can find for this creamy mousse, flavored like a Creamsicle with natural ingredients from the garden.   *Serves 4*

1 ripe Charentais melon
   (or ½ ripe small cantaloupe)

1 tablespoon honey

2 teaspoons finely chopped fresh mint

Pinch salt

½ teaspoon powdered gelatin

¾ cup heavy cream

1 pint fresh strawberries, stemmed and sliced, plus 4 small whole strawberries for garnish

1 Cut the melon in half and scoop the flesh from the rind, discarding the seeds. Purée the flesh in a food processor or blender. You should have 1 cup of purée.

2 Combine the purée, honey, mint, and salt in a medium saucepan and sprinkle the gelatin on top. Let stand until the gelatin softens, about 5 minutes. Cook over medium-low heat, stirring constantly, until the gelatin dissolves, about 3 minutes. Do not let the purée come to a boil; just gently simmer, adjusting the heat as needed. Transfer to a medium bowl. Refrigerate, stirring often, until the purée is cool but not set, about 1 hour.

3 In a chilled medium bowl, whip the cream with an electric mixer on high until stiff peaks form. Fold the cream into the purée. Spoon into four wine glasses, alternating with layers of the sliced strawberries. Cover with plastic wrap and refrigerate until chilled and lightly set, for at least 2 and up to 8 hours. Serve chilled, topping each parfait with a small strawberry.

The Four Friends Garden
Sharing Squares

Garden Personality: *A patchwork quilt symbolizes friendship; likewise, in this garden each of the four squares reflects the unique personality of one of the four gardeners, and all the squares blend together as one. Inspired by the concept of a community garden, the Four Friends Garden offers camaraderie, recreation, and education, with a common goal of growing nutritious food.*

Planning your garden around the kitchen table can lead to a wish list of seeds and plants far larger than a single family can possibly use. If your family garden has grown too large, perhaps it's time to invite friends to share not just seeds, but also garden tools, fencing materials, and creativity in a healthy shared activity.

The Four Friends Garden is a great way to create mutual ownership and encourage harmony among friends. Furthermore, it makes practical sense to combine seed orders, share garden tools, and provide incentive to each other along the way. In a group effort, each friend can choose a single plot and become the steward of its plants for the whole group to share. One friend could be in charge of growing all the tomato, eggplant, and fruiting crops, while another could take responsibility for lettuce and salad greens. A third friend might choose to tend the onions, carrots, and beets, and the fourth could manage the beans, peas, and potatoes. This way, a full spectrum of plants could be grown in a single garden, with everyone benefiting from the care and expertise that each gardener brings to the whole, and all can share in the harvest.

Ten Tips for Growing a Four Friends Garden

1 Put together a group order for seeds and plants.

2 Surround the garden with edible fruits: raspberries, blueberries, and asparagus.

3 Build a tool shed for a communal set of garden tools and invest in a wheelbarrow.

4 Visit a community garden to see how plots are arranged, and set up general guidelines that can be agreed upon.

5 Invite families with small children to participate and learn from each other.

6 Add a picnic table in order to share lunch or potluck dinner with each other.

7 Follow the four-square organic rotation system to keep the crops revolving clockwise around the garden.

8 Designate a member of your garden club to tend a single plant group for the benefit of all.

9 Divide the harvest evenly, sharing equally in the success and failures of the garden.

10 Build a communal kitchen to preserve your harvest together. Learn the techniques for freezing, canning, and cold storage in a root cellar.

OVERALL SIZE: *40 feet by 24 feet*
BED SIZE: *(4) 8 feet by 10 feet*
PATH WIDTH: *4 feet*
BORDER: *4-foot perennial bed outside fence*
RAISED BED: *Rough hewn cedar or logs*
PATH MATERIAL: *Small white pea stone*
FENCE: *White picket fence*

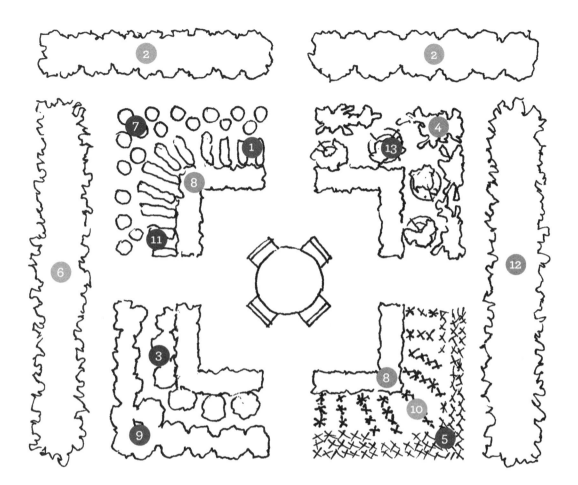

Four Friends Garden Plant List

1. Basil: Sweet Genovese, Red Rubin, and Thai
2. Blueberries
3. Bush Beans: Provider (green), Rocdor (Yellow), and Royal Burgundy (purple)
4. Cucumbers: Lemon and Orient Express
5. Dill: Fernleaf and Dukat
6. Golden raspberries
7. Lettuce: Loose-leaf Cutting Mix and Mixed Head
8. Nasturtium
9. Rhubarb
10. Shallots: French Demi-Long
11. Spinach: Space
12. Strawberries
13. Tomatoes: Sungold, Brandywine, and San Marzano

2 Blueberries

Blueberries make a good fruit crop for home gardens since they require small space, yet the plants require highly acidic soil conditions for best results. Few backyard soils are naturally acidic enough to grow quality blueberries. Research the best varieties for your climate. Blueberry plants begin to produce fruit in their third season; however, they do not become fully productive for about six years. Once in production, test soil for pH and make adjustments as necessary for highest yields. Cover with netting to provide protection from birds.

7 Lettuce: Mixed Head Types

Lettuce is classified in four basic groups: head, loose-leaf, romaine, and butter crunch. Seeds can be direct sowed in a single row or in a block design; allow 6 inches between heads. For best results, start seeds in plug trays and transplant into the garden when 3 inches tall and a good root system is in place. Keep plants watered and harvest with scissors when heads are formed and before a seed shoot develops in the center, which makes the lettuce bitter in flavor. Lettuce seed does best in cool weather, and seed will not germinate in temperatures higher than 70°F. Plan to plant a variety for a full range of color, form, and flavor. Favorites: Matchless, Four Seasons, Red Butterworth, Oliver, Little Gem, Red Grenoble, Craquerelle du Midi, Reine des Glaces, Oakleaf.

11 Spinach

Spinach prefers the cool weather of early spring and late fall, and provides dark, leafy greens that are adaptable to many delicious recipes. Several types of spinach are available, consisting of smooth or crinkly leaves, and each will have a different degree of heat tolerance, so be sure to select the best match for your climate. The smooth leaves are best for salads, while the crinkly leaves are excellent served lightly steamed or in recipes. Direct sow seeds in the garden in prepared loose soil. Seeds can be planted tightly in a single row or broadcast in a block; allow 5 inches between rows in order to cultivate. Keep plants watered and harvest with scissors when leaves reach about 5 inches in height and before flower heads are formed. Favorites: Space, Regiment, Indian Summer.

13 Tomatoes

Focus on heirloom varieties that offer you a range of colors and flavors that go beyond the ordinary. Prestart seeds in individual small pots four to six weeks before the frost-free date and transplant when temperatures are steadily above freezing. Mulch the base of the plants with straw to prevent water from splashing soil onto the bottom leaves, which can cause soil-borne disease. Keep suckers trimmed to just the branches that have fruit. Favorites: Sun Gold Cherry, Red or Green Zebra, Persimmon, Big Rainbow, Garden Peach, Brandywine.

Rhubarb Streusel

Rhubarb, a reliable perennial, rewards the gardener with ample fruit from early spring until the end of strawberry season, and if you are especially lucky it can continue all summer. Especially good as a morning treat or with afternoon tea, this recipe balances the tart nature of rhubarb with a sweet crumb topping. To preserve rhubarb for winter use, simply remove the leaves, chop the stalks into 1-inch pieces, and freeze in self-sealing bags. *Serves 10*

1¼ cups milk

1 tablespoon cider vinegar

2¼ cups unbleached
    all-purpose flour

1 teaspoon baking soda

1 teaspoon sea salt

8 tablespoons (1 stick) unsalted butter,
    at room temperature

1¼ cups packed light or dark brown sugar

1 large egg

¼ cup plain yogurt

3 cups rhubarb, leaves removed,
    sliced ½ inch thick

TOPPING

½ cup packed light or dark brown sugar

½ cup old-fashioned rolled oats

1½ teaspoons ground cinnamon

1 Position a rack in the center of the oven and preheat to 350°F. Lightly butter and flour a 9-by-13-inch baking pan, tapping out the excess flour.

2 Combine the milk and vinegar and let stand until the milk curdles, about 5 minutes. In a separate bowl, mix the flour, baking soda, and salt to combine.

3 In the medium bowl of an electric blender, cream the butter and brown sugar together until light and fluffy, about 3 minutes. Beat in the egg and the yogurt. Gradually add the milk and flour mixtures in alternation until both are incorporated. Fold in the rhubarb to blend. Spread the batter evenly in the pan.

4 In a small bowl, mix together the topping ingredients and sprinkle over the batter.

5 Bake for 35–45 minutes. Cool the pan on a wire rack and serve warm or at room temperature.

Romaine Lettuce with Zesty Parmesan Vinaigrette

This creamy dressing for a classic Caesar salad will match the quality of your own homegrown romaine lettuce, topped with pesto croutons, thin slices of red torpedo onions, and slices of grilled chicken. Pep it up with extra garlic or pepper for a spicier version to match the flavor of the greens. *Serves 4*

1 teaspoon Dijon mustard

Zest and juice of 1 lemon

1 large clove garlic, minced

1 egg yolk

1 tablespoon water

½ cup extra virgin olive oil

1 teaspoon freshly ground pepper

1 tablespoon freshly grated Parmigiano-Reggiano cheese

2 heads baby romaine lettuce

1 small sweet red onion, thinly sliced

½ cup Pesto Croutons (see below)

2 tablespoons finely chopped Italian flat-leaf parsley

1 cup finely sliced grilled chicken (optional)

1 Prepare the dressing: In a blender, combine the mustard, lemon zest and juice, garlic, egg yolk, and water. With the blender running, pour in a slow stream of olive oil. Transfer to a small bowl and season with the pepper and cheese.

2 Rinse the romaine and pat dry. Slice the heads in half lengthwise (top to bottom) to reveal the hearts. Place one half on each of four chilled salad plates. Drizzle with the dressing. Garnish with the onions, croutons, parsley, and grilled chicken, if using.

Pesto Croutons

These croutons are delicious on salads, in soups, or just as a snack. *Makes 1 cup*

4 slices thick French bread

1 tablespoon Basil Pesto (see page 102)

Preheat the oven to 375°F. Cut the bread into ½-inch cubes. In a small bowl, toss together the pesto and bread cubes, pressing the pesto into the bread cubes with the back of a spoon or your fingers. Spread the cubes in a single layer on a baking sheet and bake for 15 minutes, turning once, until lightly toasted and crisp.

Fall Spinach with Spicy Mediterranean Vinaigrette

Mellow greens like butterhead lettuce balance the more piquant spinach and mustard greens that are abundant in the fall. I love to add a sidekick of Crispy Chinese Walnuts, which can also serve as a nice appetizer. *Serves 4*

2 cups fresh red Osaka mustard greens

3 cups spinach leaves

1 head butterhead lettuce

½ clove garlic

Pinch salt

¼ cup Spicy Mediterranean Vinaigrette (see below), to taste

2 hard-boiled eggs, peeled and chopped

½ sweet red onion, thinly sliced

¼ cup Crispy Chinese Walnuts (see facing page)

1 Wash and carefully dry the mustard greens, spinach, and lettuce. Wrap the greens in a tea towel and refrigerate until ready to use.

2 Season a wooden salad bowl by rubbing with the garlic and salt. Toss. Add the greens, and spoon over the dressing, to taste. Add the eggs, onions, and walnuts, and then toss again.

Spicy Mediterranean Vinaigrette *Makes ¼ cup*

⅛ teaspoon ground cumin

¼ teaspoon ground coriander

½ teaspoon black mustard seed

½ cup carrot juice

2 tablespoons golden raisins

2 tablespoons red wine vinegar

4 sprigs fresh cilantro

1 tablespoon plain yogurt

1 teaspoon honey

½ tablespoon red pepper flakes

¼ cup extra virgin olive oil

Sea salt and freshly ground black pepper, to taste

1 In a dry skillet, heat the cumin, coriander, and mustard seeds over medium heat until fragrant, 2–3 minutes. Add the carrot juice and simmer over medium heat until reduced by half.

2 Place the raisins in a blender and pour the hot juice over them, allowing them to plump for 5 minutes before adding the remaining ingredients, except the oil, salt, and pepper, to the blender.

3 With the blender running, gradually add the oil and blend for 1 minute, until smooth. Season with salt and pepper.

Crispy Chinese Walnuts *Makes 1 cup*

1 cup walnut halves

⅛ cup salt

¼ cup safflower oil

⅛ cup sugar

1 tablespoon red pepper flakes

1 Drop the walnut halves into a quart of boiling water. Return to a boil and turn off the heat. Allow to sit for 2 minutes.

2 Scoop off the scum, and drain the walnuts into a colander. Toss with the salt.

3 In a skillet, heat the oil over medium high heat. Add the walnuts, spread in a single layer, and cook, stirring frequently, until golden, 5–10 minutes. Transfer to the colander and drain the oil.

4 Sprinkle with the sugar and red pepper flakes while still hot. Toss to completely coat, and cool before serving.

Tomato Maple Salsa

Hot, sweet, and spicy, this salsa is just right for snacking with chips or smothering a tortilla. Keep chunky for burst of flavor and bright color. This salsa is best when served fresh, but large batches can be preserved in canning jars following the proper guidelines for canning tomatoes.
Makes 6 cups

6 medium ripe tomatoes (about 4 pounds)

2 sweet peppers

2 medium onions, finely diced

1 habanero

1 jalapeño

2 cloves garlic, minced

¼ cup chopped fresh dill

¼ cup chopped fresh cilantro

¼ cup chopped fresh Italian flat-leaf parsley

Juice of 1 lemon

Juice of 1 lime

1 teaspoon sea salt

1 teaspoon ground cumin

⅓ cup pure maple syrup

2 tablespoons soy sauce

1 Trim the tops off the tomatoes and gently squeeze out the juice and seeds from the interior cavities. Discard the insides and coarsely chop the tomato flesh into ½-inch pieces. There should be about 5 cups of chopped tomatoes. Set aside in a large bowl.

2 Slice the sweet peppers in half; remove the stem ends and seeds. Coarsely chop and add to the tomatoes, along with the chopped onions. With a paring knife, trim the tops off the habanero and the jalapeño, slice the peppers in half, and remove the seeds. (Be careful not to touch your eyes or your face when handling the peppers, and clean the cutting board, the knife, and your hands carefully when you're done.) Slice and mince and add them to the tomatoes, sweet peppers, and onions. Add the garlic to the mixture.

3 Add the herbs, lemon juice, lime juice, salt, and cumin; then pour in the maple syrup and soy sauce. Mix together well, taste, and adjust seasoning. The salsa can be used fresh or placed in the refrigerator overnight so the flavors can blend. (You may need to drain some of the liquid from the salsa that has accumulated overnight.) The salsa will keep in the refrigerator for up to 1 week.

Upside-Down Rhubarb Cake

Rhubarb emerges miraculously every spring; its leafy tops provide welcome shade for pets seeking relief from the heat. Its red stalks are so prolific that you are sure to have plenty to freeze for use throughout the year. *Serves 8*

4 tablespoons (½ stick) unsalted butter

1¼ cups packed dark brown sugar

3 cups rhubarb in ½-inch dice
(about 4 large stalks)

2 cups unbleached white all-purpose flour

1 teaspoon baking powder

¼ teaspoon baking soda

½ teaspoon ground ginger

⅛ teaspoon ground cloves

½ teaspoon ground cinnamon

½ teaspoon sea salt

¾ cup yogurt

2 large eggs

¼ cup vegetable oil

2 tablespoons finely chopped
crystallized ginger

Ginger-Infused Whipped Cream
(see page 235)

1 Position a rack in the center of the oven and preheat to 350°F.

2 In a 10-inch ovenproof skillet, preferably cast-iron, melt the butter. Stir in ½ cup of the brown sugar. Place the skillet in the oven and bake until the syrup is bubbling, about 5 minutes. Remove from the oven and spread the rhubarb in a single layer in the skillet.

3 In a medium bowl, sift together the flour, baking powder, baking soda, spices, and salt. Set aside.

4 In the bowl of an electric mixer, blend together the remaining ¾ cup brown sugar, the yogurt, eggs, oil, and ginger. Add the flour mixture slowly and blend just until smooth, taking care not to overmix. Pour over the rhubarb mixture and smooth the top.

5 Bake for about 30 minutes, or until the center of the cake springs back when pressed. Remove from the oven, and cool on a wire rack for 10 minutes.

6 Run a knife around the inside edge of the skillet. Place a serving plate over the skillet, and then invert the cake to unmold. Serve warm with the whipped cream.

Peach and Mixed Berry Cobbler

Cobblers are a great way to serve seasonal fruit. During the summer, a combination of berries and peaches celebrates one of the great culinary matches. My buttermilk biscuit topping has a touch of cardamom to accent the juicy fruit. I bake the berries first, so that the topping stays light and airy. *Serves 4 to 6*

FILLING

½ cup sugar

1 tablespoon cornstarch

⅛ teaspoon ground cinnamon

⅛ teaspoon salt

2 pints fresh blueberries

1 pint fresh raspberries or blackberries

6 ripe fresh peaches, peeled and
    sliced into sections

Grated zest and juice of 1 lemon

TOPPING

1 cup unbleached white flour

2 tablespoons cornmeal

¼ cup plus 2 teaspoons sugar,
    plus extra for sprinkling

2 teaspoons baking powder

¼ teaspoon baking soda

¼ teaspoon salt

4 tablespoons (½ stick) unsalted butter,
    melted

⅓ cup buttermilk

½ teaspoon vanilla extract

½ teaspoon ground cardamom

⅛ teaspoon ground cinnamon,
    plus extra for sprinkling

Ginger-Infused Whipped Cream
    (see facing page)

1 Preheat the oven to 375°F.

2 For the filling, stir the sugar, cornstarch, cinnamon, and salt together in a large bowl. Add the berries and peaches and mix gently until evenly coated. Stir in the lemon zest and juice and transfer to a 9-inch glass pie pan. Place the pie pan on a baking sheet and bake for 25 minutes.

3 For the topping, whisk the flour, cornmeal, ¼ cup sugar, baking powder, baking soda, and salt together in a large bowl. In a smaller bowl, whisk together the melted butter, buttermilk, and vanilla. Stir in 2 teaspoons sugar, the cardamom, and the cinnamon

and set aside. A few minutes before the hot berries emerge from the oven, assemble by adding the wet ingredients to the dry ingredients, stirring gently until the ingredients are just combined and no dry pockets remain.

4 Remove the fruit filling from the oven and raise the oven temperature to 425°F. Spoon 8 equal-size pieces of biscuit topping onto the filling, spacing them at least ½ inch apart. Sprinkle each with a little mixture of cinnamon and sugar, and bake until the filling is bubbling and the biscuit topping is golden brown and cooked through, about 15 minutes. Cool slightly before serving with the whipped cream.

Ginger-Infused Whipped Cream *Makes 1 cup*

1 cup heavy cream

1 tablespoon peeled and shredded fresh
   ginger (use the large holes on a box
   grater)

2 tablespoons sugar

In a medium saucepan over medium heat, bring the heavy cream just to a boil. Remove
from the heat and add the ginger. Cover and refrigerate until well chilled, at least 4 hours.
Strain through a wire sieve into a mixing bowl. Add the sugar and whip until the cream
is stiff.

Resources

Designing a Kitchen Garden

While garden design may look great on paper, very few of us have a perfectly flat, south-facing, well-drained yard. Take measurements, then use graph paper to block out the shapes and patterns you have planned. Use these for an imaginary walk-through before the actual work begins. Once you have settled on your final design, inspect it from all angles: from the deck, the living room, and the upstairs window looking down. How does it look from the road? Do you have sufficient privacy from your neighbors? Here are steps to follow to help you prepare your garden and take your design from paper into reality.

ORIENTATION

Vegetables are sun lovers. Find a place on the south side of your house and explore all the views both inside and outside the house. If the land slopes, build a retaining wall and backfill to create level ground. How will natural foot traffic affect the location of the garden? Where does the water drain after a heavy rainstorm? What direction does the wind blow when a storm comes through? Could you create a welcoming herb garden in place of the traditional shrubbery near your home's entrance?

BEDS

There are two main choices in building garden beds: elevated or raised beds, or beds at ground level. What you choose will largely depend on your preference. The garden beds should be no wider than four feet, or the distance you can reach across with your arm. For wider beds, provide stepping stones or boards to keep foot traffic contained and avoid soil compaction.

PATHS

Paths are the bones of the garden. They hold together the design and establish the character of the garden. It is important to set up the paths between the beds in a practical design that allows easy movement for the gardener and enough room to turn a wheelbarrow. The main garden paths are ideally about four-feet wide, while the auxiliary paths can be narrower, even just wide enough for a stepping stone or for single-foot traffic to get into the beds for weeding. Plan paths with easy access to the compost pile and toolshed, because these will be essential to your daily routine.

PLANT MATERIALS

Select a range of different plants that give you a long season of harvest, which will include early spring peas, as well as late season broccoli and cabbage. Fast-growing summer crops can be harvested and replanted throughout the season, so try to allow room to keep those growing successively; slower-growing crops take more time to mature. Group plants according to height and soil requirements, as well as color, to create a visually engaging garden. Plan to rotate crops each season to keep the soil healthy and rejuvenated.

CREATE COMFORT

Establishing areas for relaxing under a shade tree, or enjoying a meal outdoors is one of the great pleasures of an edible garden. Be sure to include benches, ornamental trees, and objets d'art that reflect your personal style. No room for a tree? Build a shade arbor or a trellis, and plant trees around the perimeter of the garden to establish boundaries between the lawn and the garden.

Preserving the Bounty

In the fall, I reach for my faithful preserving kettle and set a brine of vinegar and spices to simmer on top of the stove. Bags of sugar, ginger knobs, and red-skinned garlic clutter my counter next to an army of clean jars and lids. Fruit is chopped and stirred with a wooden spoon as everything simmers and the kitchen fills with a spicy aroma. The first canning session of the year is like learning how to drive on ice; it's a little tricky at first, but once I remember how to do it, I don't want to stop.

If you aren't already a dedicated canner, it is well worth learning. Follow a recipe for the correct proportions of ingredients and timing for the cooking process. The joys of food preservation are most appreciated in the middle of winter, yet I take pride year round in the jars that adorn my pantry shelf. A flavorful chutney or pickle heightens a winter menu with a sweet and sour burst, while a zesty salsa from a late summer explosion of tomatoes and chiles transports me back into the garden.

ESSENTIAL EQUIPMENT FOR CANNING

* **A heavy-bottomed steel or enameled pot** with a lid will cook acidic foods such as tomatoes or chutneys without picking up the flavor of the metal—a danger when cooking with aluminum pots. The heavy bottom discourages scorching.

* **Canning rack and jar holder** to transfer and lift the jars in and out of the water when hot-pack processing jars.

* **Canning funnel** with a wide mouth is essential to pour ingredients neatly into the jars without a mess.

* **Canning jars** must be spotlessly clean, without any cracks or nicks. Select jars that are specifically for canning, and do not reuse jars from commercially processed foods, such as mayonnaise or jam.

* **Canning bands and lids** must have no dents and be rust free. Because the lids are not reusable (the heat destroys the seal) purchase new canning lids every time; however, you can reuse the rims.

* **Labels** can be homemade or bought pre-printed, but always remember to label your jars with the ingredients and the date.

1 Wash the canning jars and lids in hot, soapy water and rinse well before sterilizing. If you use a dishwasher to do the job, you won't have to sterilize the jars in a kettle of boiling water as long as you use the jars while they are piping hot.

2 Sterilize the jars in a pot of boiling water or in the dishwasher while the preserves are cooking. Remember, the jars must be piping hot when you add the preserves. Heat is an important factor in canning, and the preserves must be boiling hot when placed in the hot, sterilized jars.

3 To sterilize the jars, fill a canning pot (or any large pot) about two-thirds full with water and bring to a boil over high heat. Place the clean jars in a canning rack, and submerge in the boiling water for 10 minutes. Remove the jars from the pot, and invert them onto a clean tea towel until ready to fill.

4 Place the lids with rubber seals in a bowl and cover with boiling water. Do not boil the rims in a saucepan, or the rubber seals will soften too much.

5 Using a canning funnel, spoon the hot preserves into the hot jars, leaving 1/4-inch of space at the top. With a hot, wet towel, carefully wipe any spills from the rim of each jar. Attach the lids and bands, and lightly screw them on to secure, but not too tight. Invert the jars on a thick towel or kitchen counter and let cool for 10 minutes. Set them upright and allow them to cool completely before applying labels. Store in a cool, dark place until ready to use.

6 When a recipe requires a hot water bath, this means returning the jars to the canning pot to cook. Fill a canning pot two-thirds full of water and bring to a full boil over high heat. Place the jars in a canning rack and lower them into the water. Add enough boiling water to cover the jars by 1 inch. Return to a boil, and process for the length of time directed in the recipe—typically 10–20 minutes. Start counting from the time the water re-boils, not from when you place the jars in the water. Lift the jars out of the pot and place on a towel or wire rack, allowing the jars to cool completely before applying labels. Store in a cool, dark place until ready to use.

Beyond canning, there is another way of preserving the bounty: freezing. Learning what vegetables are best to freeze, and also how to freeze them properly to retain flavor and vitamin content, is essential for success. The temperature in your freezer will fluctuate whenever the door is opened, so try to minimize the number of times you open the freezer. The ideal freezer temperature is 0°F or lower. If you are serious about freezing produce, it is worth the money to buy a free-standing deep freezer rather than depend on the freezer compartment of your refrigerator. Purchase a freezer thermometer to monitor the temperature; uneven temperature will encourage moisture to form inside the containers and cause dreaded freezer burn.

A Well-stocked Pantry

I love color; my living room is painted tomato red, my dining room sunflower yellow, and the food I serve is accented with brilliant edible flowers and emerald green herbs harvested fresh from my kitchen garden. Cooking and gardening naturally go hand in hand, and it is key to take time to enjoy both activities, but I'll admit that sometimes I come in after a long day of clipping, digging, and weeding and find myself simply too exhausted to cook. When you cook from the garden, the stars of the show are your own homegrown ingredients, but behind the scenes are key supporting actors. Stock your pantry with these essential items before the season starts, reduce trips to the grocery store, and let inspiration come from your kitchen garden.

The Pantry Shelves

Stock up before the season starts to reduce extra trips to the grocery store, but remember to rotate your inventory to keep flavors fresh.

1. Extra virgin olive oil
2. Assorted vinegars for salad dressing
3. Real lemons
4. Summer: fresh herbs
5. Winter: dried fresh herbs and spices
6. Vanilla bean
7. Real Parmigiano-Reggiano
8. Tomato paste
9. Grains: rice, barley, quinoa, bulgur
10. Vermont maple syrup
11. Bacon or prosciutto
12. Walnuts, pignoli (pine nuts)
13. Crystallized ginger
14. Dried lentils and other legumes
15. Dried wild mushrooms
16. Onions, potatoes, squash (in season)
17. Garlic, onions, shallots
18. Soy or tamari sauce, fish sauce
19. Capers, olives, anchovies
20. Miso paste
21. Vegetable bouillon concentrate
22. Dijon mustard
23. Coarse sea salt, kosher pickling salt, Fleur de Sel, grey salt
24. Black peppercorns and pepper grinder
25. Flour: whole wheat, white bread, and semolina

Recipe Index

Aioli, 206

Almond Topping, Apple Crisp with, 135

Amaretto Cream-Cheese Crust, Pumpkin Tart with, 92–93

Apple Crisp with Almond Topping, 135

Applesauce, Simple Homemade, 132

Artichokes Stuffed with Herbed Bread Crumbs, 121

Arugula:
Arugula and Mint Thai Soup, 44
Arugula and Roasted Pear Salad, 159
Arugula Pesto with Herbed Ricotta Gnocchi, 162–63
Arugula Salad with Lemon Vinaigrette, 189

Asparagus:
Asparagus Soup with Coconut Lemon Crème, 202
Asparagus with Lemon Chive Sauce, 161

Bacon: Spinach Salad with Warm Bacon Dressing, 173

Basil:
Basil Pesto, 102
Basil Pesto Swirl Bread, 203
Basil-Wrapped Grilled Fish, 103
blanching and freezing, 103
Golden Tomato Gazpacho with Basil, 172
Lemon Basil Dressing, 75

Beans:
Bean and Potato Salad with Warm Mustard Vinaigrette, 204
Borlotti Bean and Kale Soup, 145

Beef:
Strip Steak with Garlic Scapes, 205

Beets:
Beets and Greens with Aioli, 206
Rainbow Beet Soufflé, 176
Roasted Beet and Walnut Salad, 217

Berries: Peach and Mixed Berry Cobbler, 234

Bisque, Butternut Squash, 188

Blueberry-Zucchini Bread, 89

Borlotti Bean and Kale Soup, 145

Breads:
Baked Herb Croutons, 161
Basil Pesto Swirl Bread, 203
Blueberry-Zucchini Bread, 89
Corn and Jalapeño Muffins, 131
Golden Focaccia with Savory Onion Confit, 186–87
Herbed Bread Crumbs, 121
Lemon Ricotta Fritters with Lavender Honey, 107
Parmesan Herb Popovers, 102
Pesto Croutons, 229
Rosemary Croutons, 116
Summer-Herb Cheese Bread, 106

Brussels Sprouts, Glazed Spiced Pecans with, 120

Butternut Squash Bisque, 188

Cakes:
Upside-Down Rhubarb Cake, 233
Vermont Carrot Cake with Maple Frosting, 192

Cape Gooseberry Clafoutis, 207

Caponata, Eggplant, 134

Caramelized Onion Tart, 216

Caramelized Shallot Custard, 191

Carrots:
Carrot and Tarragon Tart, 61
Ginger Carrot Soup with Creamy Lime Garnish, 88
Roasted Carrots with Cippolini Onions, 149

Vermont Carrot Cake with Maple Frosting, 192

Chard:
Rainbow Chard Enchiladas, 78
Rainbow Chard Soup with Rosemary, 116
Wilted Chard with Ginger-Lime Tuna Steaks, 64

Cheese:
Arugula Pesto with Herbed Ricotta Gnocchi, 162–63
Cheddar Cheese Tart Crust, 118–19
Herb Cheese Spread, 105
Honey Blue Cheese Dressing, 45
Lemon Ricotta Fritters with Lavender Honey, 107
Parmesan Herb Popovers, 102
Romaine Lettuce with Zesty Parmesan Vinaigrette, 229
Summer-Herb Cheese Bread, 106
Tarragon Chicken Salad with Creamy Blue Cheese Dressing, 104
Warm Spinach and Vermont Cheddar Custard, 133

Chicken:
Mache and Chicken Salad with Lemon Tahini Dressing, 46
Tarragon Chicken Salad with Creamy Blue Cheese Dressing, 104

Chilled Lemon Cucumber Soup, 144

Chinese Walnuts, Crispy, 231

Chives: Asparagus with Lemon Chive Sauce, 161

Chutney, Ginger Peach, 77

Cilantro: Corn, Cucumber, and Cilantro Salad, 146

Clafoutis, Cape Gooseberry, 207

Cobbler: Peach and Mixed Berry Cobbler, 234

Coconut:
Asparagus Soup with Coconut Lemon Crème, 202
Braised Winter Greens with Coconut and Curry, 148

Coriander: Insalata di Misticanza with Coriander-Spiked Salmon, 48

Corn:
Corn, Cucumber, and Cilantro Salad, 146
Corn and Jalapeño Muffins, 131

Creamed Kohlrabi, 76

Creamy Blue Cheese Dressing, 105
Tarragon Chicken Salad with, 104

Creamy Tomato Dressing, 49
Dandelion Tortellini Salad with, 47

Crispy Chinese Walnuts, 231

Croutons, see Breads

Cucumbers:
Chilled Lemon Cucumber Soup, 144
Corn, Cucumber, and Cilantro Salad, 146
Herbed Cucumber Vinaigrette, 160
Quick and Easy Cucumber Dill Pickles, 177
Spicy Mesclun with Herbed Cucumber Vinaigrette, 160

Curry: Braised Winter Greens with Coconut and Curry, 148

Custards, savory:
Caramelized Shallot Custard, 191
Warm Spinach and Vermont Cheddar Custard, 133

Dandelion Tortellini Salad with Creamy Tomato Dressing, 47
Dill Pickles, Quick and Easy Cucumber, 177

Eggplant Caponata, 134
Enchiladas, Rainbow Chard, 78

Fall Spinach with Spicy Mediterranean Vinaigrette, 230
Fall Vegetable Tart, Roasted, 118–19

Fennel:
Fennel Tomato Soup, 130
Fresh Fennel Salsa over Herb-Crusted Haddock, 91

Fire-Roasted Tomato Sauce, 147

Fish:
Baked Salmon in Phyllo with Tomato-Ginger Filling, 117
Basil-Wrapped Grilled Fish, 103
Fresh Fennel Salsa over Herb-Crusted Haddock, 91
Insalata di Misticanza with Coriander-Spiked Salmon, 48
Smoked Trout with Creamy Herbed Horseradish Dressing, 218
Stewed Leeks with Fillet of Salmon, 174
Sugar Snap Peas with Poached Scrod en Papillote, 79
Wilted Chard with Ginger-Lime Tuna Steaks, 64

Focaccia: Golden Focaccia with Savory Onion Confit, 186–87

Fritters: Lemon Ricotta Fritters with Lavender Honey, 107

Garlic:
Roasted Garlic Dressing, 65
Strip Steak with Garlic Scapes, 205

Gazpachos:
Golden Tomato Gazpacho with Basil, 172
Red Tomato Gazpacho, 74

Ginger:
Baked Salmon in Phyllo with Tomato-Ginger Filling, 117
Ginger Carrot Soup with Creamy Lime Garnish, 88
Ginger-Infused Whipped Cream, 235
Ginger-Lime Vinaigrette, 65
Ginger Peach Chutney, 77
Leg of Lamb Infused with Rosemary and Ginger, 190
Wilted Chard with Ginger-Lime Tuna Steaks, 64

Glazed Spiced Pecans with Brussels Sprouts, 120

Glazed Vermont Quail, 175

Gnocchi: Arugula Pesto with Herbed Ricotta Gnocchi, 162–63

Golden Tomato Gazpacho with Basil, 172

Grilled foods:
Basil-Wrapped Grilled Fish, 103

Romaine and Radicchio with Honey Blue Cheese Dressing, 45

Haddock: Fresh Fennel Salsa over Herb-Crusted Haddock, 91

Herbs:
Artichokes Stuffed with Herbed Bread Crumbs, 121
Arugula Pesto with Herbed Ricotta Gnocchi, 162–63
Baked Herb Croutons, 161
Fresh Fennel Salsa over Herb-Crusted Haddock, 91
Herb Cheese Spread, 105
Herbed Cucumber Vinaigrette, 160
Herb-Marinated Pork Tenderloin, 132
Lettuce and Mesclun with Herbed Vinaigrette, 63
Summer-Herb Cheese Bread, 106

Honey:
Honey Blue Cheese Dressing, 45
Lavender Honey, 107

Horseradish:
Creamy Herbed Horseradish Dressing, 218

Prepared Horseradish, 218
Insalata di Misticanza with Coriander-Spiked Salmon, 48

Kale: Borlotti Bean and Kale Soup, 145
Kohlrabi, Creamed, 76

Lamb: Leg of Lamb Infused with Rosemary and Ginger, 190
Lavender Honey, 107
Leeks:
  Leek and Potato Soup, 158
  Stewed Leeks with Fillet of Salmon, 174
Lemons:
  Asparagus Soup with Coconut Lemon Crème, 202
  Asparagus with Lemon Chive Sauce, 161
  Chilled Lemon Cucumber Soup, 144
  Lemon Ricotta Fritters with Lavender Honey, 107
  Lemon Tahini Dressing, 51
  Lemon Vinaigrette, 189
  Rainbow Tomatoes with Lemon Basil Dressing, 75
Lettuce and Mesclun with Herbed Vinaigrette, 63
Limes:
  Ginger Carrot Soup with Creamy Lime Garnish, 88
  Ginger-Lime Vinaigrette, 65

Mache and Chicken Salad with Lemon Tahini Dressing, 46
Maple syrup:
  Maple Balsamic Vinaigrette, 49
  Maple Frosting, 192
  Tomato Maple Salsa, 232
Mediterranean Vinaigrette, Spicy, 230
Melon Mousse and Strawberry

Parfait, 219
Mesclun:
  Lettuce and Mesclun with Herbed Vinaigrette, 63
  Spicy Mesclun with Herbed Cucumber Vinaigrette, 160
Mint:
  Arugula and Mint Thai Soup, 44
  Parsley Mint Pistou, 65
  Summer Squash Soup with Mint Pistou, 60
Mousse: Melon Mousse and Strawberry Parfait, 219
Muffins: Corn and Jalapeño Muffins, 131

Nuts:
  Apple Crisp with Almond Topping, 135
  Crispy Chinese Walnuts, 231
  Glazed Spiced Pecans with Brussels Sprouts, 120
  Roasted Beet and Walnut Salad, 217

Olives: Black Olive Tapenade, 119
Onions:
  Caramelized Onion Tart, 216
  Golden Focaccia with Savory Onion Confit, 186–87
  Roasted Carrots with Cippolini Onions, 149

Parfait: Melon Mousse and Strawberry Parfait, 219
Parmesan Herb Popovers, 102
Parsley Mint Pistou, 65
Peaches:
  Ginger Peach Chutney, 77
  Peach and Mixed Berry Cobbler, 234
Pears: Arugula and Roasted Pear Salad, 159
Peas: Sugar Snap Peas with Poached Scrod en Papillote, 79

Pecans: Glazed Spiced Pecans with Brussels Sprouts, 120
Peppers: Corn and Jalapeño Muffins, 131
Pesto:
  Arugula Pesto with Herbed Ricotta Gnocchi, 162–63
  Basil Pesto, 102
  Basil Pesto Swirl Bread, 203
  Pesto Croutons, 229
Pickles: Quick and Easy Cucumber Dill Pickles, 177
Pies, fruit or vegetable, 119
Popovers, Parmesan Herb, 102
Pork: Herb-Marinated Pork Tenderloin, 132
Potatoes:
  Bean and Potato Salad with Warm Mustard Vinaigrette, 204
  Leek and Potato Soup, 158
  Tricolor Scalloped Potatoes, 90
Pumpkin Tart with Amaretto Cream-Cheese Crust, 92–93

Quail, Glazed Vermont, 175

Radicchio: Grilled Romaine and Radicchio with Honey Blue Cheese Dressing, 45
Rainbow Beet Soufflé, 176
Rainbow Chard Enchiladas, 78
Rainbow Chard Soup with Rosemary, 116
Rainbow Tomatoes with Lemon Basil Dressing, 75
Rhubarb:
  Rhubarb Streusel, 228
  Upside-Down Rhubarb Cake, 233
Roasted Beet and Walnut Salad, 217
Roasted Fall Vegetable Tart, 118–19
Roasted Garlic Dressing, 65
Warm Winter Salad with, 62
Romaine:

chio with Honey Blue Cheese Dressing, 45
Romaine Lettuce with Zesty Parmesan Vinaigrette, 229
Rosemary:
Leg of Lamb Infused with Rosemary and Ginger, 190
Rainbow Chard Soup with Rosemary, 116
Rosemary Croutons, 116

Salad dressings, *see* Sauces and dressings
Salads:
Arugula and Roasted Pear Salad, 159
Arugula Salad with Lemon Vinaigrette, 189
Bean and Potato Salad with Warm Mustard Vinaigrette, 204
Corn, Cucumber, and Cilantro Salad, 146
Dandelion Tortellini Salad with Creamy Tomato Dressing, 47
Fall Spinach with Spicy Mediterranean Vinaigrette, 230
Grilled Romaine and Radicchio with Honey Blue Cheese Dressing, 45
Insalata di Misticanza with Coriander-Spiked Salmon, 48
Lettuce and Mesclun with Herbed Vinaigrette, 63
Mache and Chicken Salad with Lemon Tahini Dressing, 46
Rainbow Tomatoes with Lemon Basil Dressing, 75
Roasted Beet and Walnut Salad, 217
Romaine Lettuce with Zesty Parmesan Vinaigrette, 229
Spicy Mesclun with Herbed Cucumber Vinaigrette, 160

Spinach Salad with Warm Bacon Dressing, 173
Tarragon Chicken Salad with Creamy Blue Cheese Dressing, 104
Warm Winter Salad with Roasted Garlic Dressing, 62
Salmon:
Baked Salmon in Phyllo with Tomato-Ginger Filling, 117
Insalata di Misticanza with Coriander-Spiked Salmon, 48
Stewed Leeks with Fillet of Salmon, 174
Sauces and dressings:
Aioli, 206
Basil Pesto, 102
Black Olive Tapenade, 119
Coconut Lemon Crème, 202
Creamy Blue Cheese Dressing, 105
Creamy Herbed Horseradish Dressing, 218
Creamy Lime Garnish, 88
Creamy Tomato Dressing, 49
Fire-Roasted Tomato Sauce, 147
Fresh Fennel and Tomatillo Salsa, 91
Ginger-Lime Vinaigrette, 65
Ginger Peach Chutney, 77
Herb Cheese Spread, 105
Herbed Cucumber Vinaigrette, 160
Herbed Vinaigrette, 63
homemade dressing, 51
Honey Blue Cheese Dressing, 45
Lavender Honey, 107
Lemon Basil Dressing, 75
Lemon Chive Sauce, 161
Lemon Tahini Dressing, 51
Lemon Vinaigrette, 189
Maple Balsamic Vinaigrette, 49
Maple Frosting, 192
Parsley Mint Pistou, 65

Prepared Horseradish, 218
Roasted Garlic Dressing, 65
Rosemary and Ginger Marinade, 190
Savory Onion Confit, 186–87
Spicy Mediterranean Vinaigrette, 230
Tomato Maple Salsa, 232
Warm Bacon Dressing, 173
Warm Mustard Vinaigrette, 204
Zesty Parmesan Vinaigrette, 229
Scrod: Sugar Snap Peas with Poached Scrod en Papillote, 79
Shallots: Caramelized Shallot Custard, 191
Smoked Trout with Creamy Herbed Horseradish Dressing, 218
Sorrel-and-Spinach Tartlets, 50–51
Soufflé, Rainbow Beet, 176
Soups:
Arugula and Mint Thai Soup, 44
Asparagus Soup with Coconut Lemon Crème, 202
Borlotti Bean and Kale Soup, 145
Butternut Squash Bisque, 188
Chilled Lemon Cucumber Soup, 144
Fennel Tomato Soup, 130
Ginger Carrot Soup with Creamy Lime Garnish, 88
Golden Tomato Gazpacho with Basil, 172
Leek and Potato Soup, 158
Rainbow Chard Soup with Rosemary, 116
Red Tomato Gazpacho, 74
Summer Squash Soup with Mint Pistou, 60
Spinach:
Fall Spinach with Spicy Mediterranean Vinaigrette, 230
Sorrel-and-Spinach Tartlets, 50–51
Spinach Salad with Warm Bacon

Dressing, 173
Warm Spinach and Vermont
    Cheddar Custard, 133
Squash:
    Blueberry-Zucchini Bread, 89
    Butternut Squash Bisque, 188
    Summer Squash Soup with Mint
        Pistou, 60
Stewed Leeks with Fillet of Salmon,
    174
Strawberries:
    Fresh Strawberry Crème Tart, 193
    Melon Mousse and Strawberry
        Parfait, 219
Streusel, Rhubarb, 228
Strip Steak with Garlic Scapes, 205
Sugar Snap Peas with Poached
    Scrod en Papillote, 79
Summer-Herb Cheese Bread, 106
Summer Squash Soup with Mint
    Pistou, 60

Tapenade, Black Olive, 119
Tarragon:
    Carrot and Tarragon Tart, 61
    Tarragon Chicken Salad with
        Creamy Blue Cheese Dressing,
        104
Tarts, savory:
    Caramelized Onion Tart, 216
    Carrot and Tarragon Tart, 61

Cheddar Cheese Tart Crust,
    118–19
Pumpkin Tart with Amaretto
    Cream-Cheese Crust, 92–93
Roasted Fall Vegetable Tart,
    118–19
Sorrel-and-Spinach Tartlets,
    50–51
Tarts, sweet: Fresh Strawberry
    Crème Tart, 193
Tomatillos: Fresh Fennel and To-
    matillo Salsa, 91
Tomatoes:
    Baked Salmon in Phyllo with
        Tomato-Ginger Filling, 117
    Creamy Tomato Dressing, 49
    Fennel Tomato Soup, 130
    Fire-Roasted Tomato Sauce, 147
    Golden Tomato Gazpacho with
        Basil, 172
    Rainbow Tomatoes with Lemon
        Basil Dressing, 75
    Red Tomato Gazpacho, 74
    Tomato Maple Salsa, 232
Tortellini: Dandelion Tortellini
    Salad with Creamy Tomato
    Dressing, 47
Tricolor Scalloped Potatoes, 90
Trout: Smoked Trout with Creamy
    Herbed Horseradish Dress-
    ing, 218
Tuna: Wilted Chard with Ginger-

Lime Tuna Steaks, 64

Upside-Down Rhubarb Cake, 233

Vegetables:
    Eggplant Caponata, 134
    in pies, 119
    Roasted Fall Vegetable Tart,
        118–19
Vermont Carrot Cake with Maple
    Frosting, 192
Vermont Quail, Glazed, 175

Walnuts:
    Crispy Chinese Walnuts, 231
    Roasted Beet and Walnut Salad,
        217
Whipped Cream, Ginger-Infused,
    235
Winter Greens, Braised, with Coco-
    nut and Curry, 148
Winter Salad, Warm, with Roasted
    Garlic Dressing, 62

Zesty Parmesan Vinaigrette, 229
Zucchini, Blueberry-Zucchini
    Bread, 89

Plant Index

Amaranth, 113
Anise, 155
Apple trees, espaliered, 196
Artichokes, 113, 114, 127, 155
Arugula, 41, 42
Asparagus, 179, 196, 199, 200

Basil, 100, 170
    Fino Verde, 183, 199
    Lemon, 41
    Mammoth, 71, 99
    Red Rubin, 41, 113, 169, 199, 225
    Sweet Genovese, 41, 57, 71, 99,
        113, 183, 213, 225
    Thai, 225
Beans, 209, 213
    Bush, 57, 58, 142, 183, 199, 225

Fava, 113
Hyacinth (ornamental), 85, 155,
    156
Lima, 141
Pole, 16, 58, 127, 142, 199
Shelling, 141
    Trionfo Violetto, 16, 71
Bee balm, 99
Beets, 71, 200, 209, 213, 214
Blueberries, 85, 179, 196, 225, 226
Borage, 99, 113, 155, 156
Broccoli, 113, 114, 141
Brussels sprouts, 113, 114

Cabbage, 141, 199, 201
Calendula, 57, 113, 155, 156–57
Cape gooseberries, 201

Carrots, 57, 58–59, 85, 141, 183, 199,
    209
Carthamus (Safflower), 155
Cauliflower, 213
Chard, 57, 59, 71, 113
Chervil, 41, 68, 209, 213
Chicory, 141, 143
Chives, 71, 72, 99, 169
Cilantro, 99, 100
Claytonia, 37, 41
Collards, 115, 213
Cress, 41
Cucumbers, 71, 141, 142, 209, 210,
    225

Dahlias, 213
Dill, 71, 99, 100, 209, 225

Eggplant, 127, 128
Endive, 141, 143
Eucalyptus, 155

Fennel, 113, 115, 127, 141

Garlic, 57, 199, 201
Grass, 155

Herbs, 71, 72, 95, 96, 127, 183, 213
Hollyhock, 156

Kale, 71, 113, 115

Lavender, 99, 127, 128, 156
Leeks, 57, 169, 170, 213
Lemon grass, 127
Lemon verbena, 169
Lettuce, 41, 57, 68, 85, 113, 127, 183,
    184, 199, 209, 213, 225, 226
Lovage, 72

Mache, 41, 42
Marigolds, 85, 86, 127, 155, 156, 157,
    169, 199, 209
Marjoram, 71, 99
Melons, 85, 86, 141, 213, 214
Mesclun, 41, 43, 57, 68, 71, 183, 184
Mint, 72
Monarda, 156
Mustard greens, 37, 68

Nasturtiums, 16, 41, 113, 128–29,
    156, 157, 225
  Empress of India, 183, 199
  Moonlight, 199
  Peach Melba, 183
  Whirlybird, 169, 183
Nigella, 155, 156

Onions, 57, 85, 141, 143, 183, 185,
    199, 209
Oregano, 72

Pansy, 156
Parsley, 71, 72, 99, 169, 213
Peas, 72–73, 210
  Carouby d'Maussane Snow Peas,
    113
  Green Arrow, 141
  Organ Giant, 57
  Sugar Snap, 71, 85, 86–87, 183
Peppers, 129, 170–71
  Cayenne Hot, 71
  Jalapeño, 169
  Serrano, 127, 169
  Sweet Chocolate, 183
  Thai Hot, 127
Potatoes, 57, 87, 213
Pumpkins, 85
Purslane, Goldgelber, 41

Radicchio, 41, 43
Radishes, 213, 215
Raspberries, 225
Rhubarb, 179, 213, 215, 225
Rosemary, 71, 72, 99, 101, 169

Safflower (Carthamus), 155
Sage, 72, 101, 127
Salvia, 155
Savory, summer, 71, 99
Shallots, 185, 225
Snapdragon, 57
Sorrel, 41, 43
Spinach, 41, 85, 127, 129, 183, 225,
    227
Squash, 57, 59, 183
Strawberries, 179, 225

Alpine, 71, 72
Mixed Everlasting, 85
Sunflowers, 87, 156, 210, 213
  Chocolate, 199
  Italian White, 155
  Joker, 113
  Teddy Bear, 85
  Valentine, 57
  Velvet Queen, 141
  Zebulon, 199

Tarragon, 71, 72, 99, 101, 169
Thyme, 71, 72, 99, 127, 169
Tomatillos, 199, 201
Tomatoes, 73, 171, 209, 227
  Balcony, 127
  Big Rainbow, 71, 141
  Brandywine, 225
  Cherokee Purple, 213
  Cherry, 85, 169
  Garden Peach, 57, 141, 183
  Green Zebra, 57, 71, 213
  Heirloom, 143
  Pear, 169, 213
  Persimmon, 57, 71, 141, 183
  San Marzano, 141, 225
  Sun Gold, 71, 225

Viola, 155

Zinnia, 57, 213

Index

Artist's Garden, 195–207
   design, 197, 199
   garden personality, 195
   plant list, 199–201
   recipes, 202–7
   tips for growing, 196

Beds, 238
Bell, Ilona, 195
Benches, 32
Boxwood hedges, 28

Canning, 240–41
Chef's Garden, 165–77
   design, 166, 167, 169
   garden personality, 165
   plant list, 169–71
   recipes, 172–77
   tips for growing, 166
Chickens, 180
Children's Garden, 81–93
   design, 83, 85
   garden personality, 81
   plant list, 85–87
   recipes, 88–93
   tips for growing, 82
Clay, 18
Comfort, 239
Companion planting, 209
Compost, 20
   Cold Slow Method, 20
   Hot Fast Method, 20
Cook's Garden, 67–79
   design, 69, 71
   garden personality, 67
   plant list, 71–73
   recipes, 74–79
   tips for growing, 68
Country Garden, 209–19
   design, 211, 213
   garden personality, 209
   plant list, 213–15
   recipes, 216–19
   tips for growing, 210

Culinary Herb Garden, 95–107
   design, 97, 99
   garden personality, 95
   plant list, 99–101
   recipes, 102–7
   tips for growing, 96

Deer fences, 28

Evergreen hedges, 28

Family Garden, 179–93
   design, 181, 183
   garden personality, 179
   plant list, 183–85
   recipes, 186–93
   tips for growing, 180
Fences, 28
Fertilizer, 24
Flea beetles, 38
Four Friends Garden, 221–35
   design, 223, 225
   garden personality, 221
   plant list, 225–27
   recipes, 228–35
   tips for growing, 222
Four-square design, 53, 54, 221
Freezing foods, 242

Garnish Garden, 151–63
   design, 153, 155
   garden personality, 151
   plant list, 155–57
   recipes, 158–63
   tips for growing, 152
Gates, 32
Germination, 22

Hedges, 28
Heirloom Maze Garden, 137–49
   design, 139, 141
   garden personality, 137
   plant list, 141–43
   recipes, 144–49

   tips for growing, 138
Honeybees, 30, 96

Inoculants, 86–87

Journal, keeping, 54

Kitchen gardens:
   designing, 238–39
   getting started, 16–17
   in history, 14–15

Loam, sandy, 18

Maintenance, 26
Mulch, 26

Nitrogen (N), 24
N-P-K fertilizers, 24

Organic Rotation Garden, 53–65
   design, 55, 57
   garden personality, 53
   plant list, 57–59
   recipes, 60–65
   tips for growing, 54
Orientation, 238

Paint Box Garden, 109–21
   design, 111, 113
   garden personality, 109
   plant list, 113–15
   recipes, 116–21
   tips for growing, 110
Pantry, 243
Paradise garden, 14
Paths, 239
Patio Garden, 123–35
   design, 125, 127
   garden personality, 123
   plant list, 127–29
   recipes, 130–35
   tips for growing, 124
Phosphorus (P), 24

Picket fences, 28
Planting chart, 22
Plant materials, 239
Potager, 15, 67
Potassium (K), 24
Preserves, 240–42
   canning, 240–41
   freezing, 242

Raised beds, 109, 110
Russell, Chef, 165

Salad Lover's Garden, 37–51
   design, 39, 41
   garden personality, 37
   plant list, 41–43
   recipes, 44–51
   tips for growing, 38
Sandy soil, 18
Seeds, 22
Soil, 18
Soil test kits, 18

Split-rail fences, 28
Style, 32
Supports and structures, 32

Tools, 30

Walls, stone, 28
Water, 26
Weeds, 26

Acknowledgments

Gardeners can always learn from other gardeners, and this book would not be possible without the collective vision of the many kitchen gardens I have had the pleasure to experience. Special thanks go to the exceptional gardeners who opened their gardens as a source of inspiration for my final designs and the photographs in this book: Ilona Bell, Annie Thorne, Robin Colburn, Jan Rogers, Susan Romano, Anna Johansen, Kim Ray, and Kit Mosheim.

A book is never born alone, and I am fortunate to have a multi-talented and supportive team who helped bring my vision to print. Ramsay Gourd, best known for his extraordinary architecture, surprised me with his outstanding watercolor illustrations that grace the pages of this book; photographer Ali Kaukas who brought each garden to life with her captivating photographs, and was never afraid to climb a tall ladder or get down on the ground to capture a unique perspective; and Chef Cameron Howard, who carefully tested my recipes and revised them to meet her high standards. Thank you to my editor Dervla Kelly and book designer Pamela Geismar, who showed remarkable dedication to this project, working extra hours to get it right. And to my agent, Colleen Mohyde, who provided the opportunity to share my passion for kitchen gardens.

Many others have influenced my appreciation for how kitchen gardens work in our lives. I wish to express gratitude to everyone at The Cook's Garden for continuing the legacy that we started in 1984. Thank you to Maddie Sobel for introducing me to the joys and benefits of bee keeping; and to market grower Andrew Knafel of Clear Brook Farm, for the early morning photos shoots at his farmstand. I credit Mark Wright, landscaper extraordinaire, for helping me sculpt my own backyard into an edible paradise and the staff at The Garden Conservancy, for organizing private garden tours for the enjoyment and benefit of gardeners everywhere.